3/83

SYNERGISTIC MANAGEMENT

SYNERGISTIC MANAGEMENT

Creating the Climate
for Superior Performance

Michael Doctoroff

 A DIVISION OF AMERICAN MANAGEMENT ASSOCIATIONS

Library of Congress Cataloging in Publication Data

Doctoroff, Michael.
  Synergistic management.

  Includes index.
  1. Communication in management. 2. Psychology,
Industrial. I. Title.
HD30.3.D62   658.4'5   77-12090
ISBN 0-8144-5445-3

Third Printing

In Loving Memory
Abraham Mordecai Doctoroff
Leo Levin

Preface

After reading this book, I am confident that you will become a better manager, discover some new ideas, and enjoy a sense of fulfillment from your newly acquired managerial professionalism. I can make this statement with confidence because the ideas that will be presented have all been tested in the real world of work. They have worked for me, and they will work for you.

From conception to publication, this book has taken four years. A frustration with ineffective management, a love of learning, an excitement with new ideas and a need to share them, and perhaps an egocentric desire to be immortalized in print all prompted me to undertake the task of writing this book despite a heavy schedule of working and teaching.

Many people have helped with the preparation of this book. First I must recognize the assistance of the AMACOM staff, principally Tom Gannon, who encouraged me to persevere in the development of my ideas, and Peter Reimold, who spent many hours working my somewhat disorganized text into more readable form. When he expressed the hope that his editing would be a synergistic effort, I knew that it would be.

I must also recognize the contribution of my immediate family. My wife and our three children encouraged me and gave me the time I needed to accomplish this undertaking. Their support was indeed a comfort during a time when I was totally committed to this effort and struggling to meet self-imposed schedules and deadlines.

A number of people provided assistance of a more academic

nature. Ron Eisen of Bausch & Lomb offered meaningful criticism of my first draft, and Harvey Edwards and Gladys Abraham of the Rochester Institute of Technology provided important insights into the mechanisms of writing. Marion Peller added helpful conceptual critiques.

I feel impelled to thank a number of professional colleagues who inspired my writing by their arguments or example. The names of Charles Krischer, Robert Shone, Bernt Hoppert, Isse Sheiman, Gene Letter, Ralph Gallo, and Dave Hoagland come to mind most readily, but the full list is much longer.

The help of a number of dedicated secretaries must also be recognized for their ability to translate my scrawled notes into typed copy. Special thanks are due to Sharon Haase, who typed the last two drafts of this book, Karen Valasco, and a Bausch & Lomb contingent comprised of Betty Verb, Theresa O'Reilly, and Helen Morrison.

Michael Doctoroff

Contents

Introduction

1

We usually generate our objectives for the coming year in November. Using a modified, yet typical, Management by Objectives technique, I sit with my staff, and we collectively decide the course that our division will pursue over the coming year. The whole process takes an hour or two.

In the next session, I meet with each staff member individually, and we develop objectives for each staff member and his group. After this, the whole staff again meets, and we modify each other's objectives until there is agreement on the chores to be accomplished during the coming fiscal period.

The staff members then return to their own groups and decide how they will achieve the agreed-upon goals. Usually in this process, inconsistencies in the primary objectives are uncovered. Another staff meeting follows, and the objectives and strategies are again modified, this time incorporating the concerns of the people in the different subgroups. This whole process takes about two months, so by the time planning is complete, the new year is ready to begin.

But in January or February a problem usually occurs. Consider a typical recent example. In January 1975, inflation coupled with a recession became an acute problem just when we had determined that there was little danger of our being affected by them. The recession hit us with its full impact, causing one of our most important customers to cancel most of the orders placed during the previous fiscal year. This constituted approximately 20' percent of our backlog. February saw the reduction of another 10 percent of backlog, the budget grew radically out of balance, and consequently, a good portion of our carefully developed plans became obsolete.

Other customers, too, were affected by the economic situation, and this had a further effect on us. As some of their businesses deteriorated, they reacted by modifying their product lines, and this required us to change our plans in concert with their new needs. Our shifts in production were complemented by changes in research and development, and pressure grew from these companies to alter our products so that they could tailor their own product lines to the new and limited market needs. The problems encountered by us during this period were complex and numerous, and they were by no means solved by the worldly system of Management by Objectives that we were using.

We had a multitude of meetings. There were meetings about everything. It sometimes seemed as if the days were a continuum of meetings. Some people were performing poorly, others had trouble meeting objectives, others were suddenly understaffed. People were brought together, and the problems were worked out to a common understanding. This was not always a smooth process. Conflicts between people and between the objectives of different groups frequently developed, and we attempted to reduce them in ten-minute sessions that were focused on the exact problem at hand.

However, in spite of all the know-it-all theory and meetings, conflict seemed to flourish. Production control hated quality control, quality control hated manufacturing, manufacturing hated marketing, and everybody hated the engineers. Something needed to be done.

For a situation like this, where conflict runs rampant, we came up with a very special solution in my division. I am sure that with all the attention to well-defined objectives, our special procedure for removing conflict might seem somewhat strange and unorthodox. But our meetings work so well at resolving conflicts that I would like to tell you how we do it. In essence, in order to fill the void created by a strong, overcompensating sense of purpose, a purposeless meeting is required.

I call such meetings on occasion. It always seems somewhat strange and uncomfortable for a student of directive management to engage in such activities; nevertheless, I do it. In fact, I go one step further and formalize the informality. Certain laws are established. The meeting is limited to one hour and to my immediate staff of four people, and there is no agenda. It is further dictated that there will be no note taking, no reporting to superiors or subordinates, and no prescribed agendas from one meeting to the next. The meeting might be scheduled periodically, for example, on Tuesday mornings at 8:30 A.M.

At the meeting, discussion starts by talk of the weather, professional disturbances, technical problems, and so on. Anybody can talk and initiate the discussion. Rather rapidly, the conversation subject seems to focus on company-oriented problems, but this is not necessary. In the past months, we have discussed in detail problems with top management, the place of our division in the organization, the inadequacies of marketing, frustrations over finances, and differences among people.

Alternatively, we might discuss the total corporate scheme. We might get involved in a discussion on the concept of growth within the corporation, or on why the chief executives consider us corporate radicals. We might pursue feelings of inadequacy, corporate trends, or more. The field for discussion is wide open.

A full enumeration of the things we have discussed would not only prove difficult in view of the prohibition of note taking, it would also read uninterestingly (for it is involved with our industrial business and not universal principles), and, most important, it would in some cases violate the privacy rights of my colleagues.

In most cases, the general consensus was that the hour's time had been well spent. After one meeting, we discovered that we had all enrolled to attend the company Christmas party. After another, we all made a point of meeting in the company cafeteria. Other effects of these discussions were equally magical. People felt better. They looked forward to the meetings.

Everyone agreed that the meeting was a good thing, even though, from a conventional perspective, nothing valuable could be considered accomplished from it. After three or four weeks of this kind of activity, it was easy to see that the tension between individuals and groups of individuals was significantly decreased.

Perhaps industrial psychologists could tell us why these meetings were felt to be valuable. Surely, they contained traces of sensitivity training, analysis, and even brainstorming. For some of these techniques, the assistance of a qualified leader is recommended, but in our sessions we found it easy to reorient discussions, without the help of a leader, when a sensitive area was touched. Still, there was enough depth to feel better, enriched, and closer. I think that we feel as we do after such meetings because they expose us to problems in an environment characterized by professional respect and discipline.

You might be encouraged to try this kind of meeting yourself. Call your staff to your office, explain the simple rules and the time limit of the session, and see to it that all the rules are observed. Silence might ensue, or an active debate may develop. You can make a tirade, or any of your subordinates may upstage you. It makes no difference. I promise you, the rewards will become evident in the very first session.

How can I make such a statement? The answer is simple. Management by Objectives, like many other formalized systems of management, is an oversimplified recipe of how to manage. With the oversimplification, certain ingredients important to the proper management of an organization, especially the interpersonal aspects of management, are ignored, and the organization loses its balance. The purposeless meeting offers an opportunity for the proper balance to be restored.

The process seems similar to what purportedly happens in an infant's diet. The infant selects those foods that are necessary in order to maintain an overall vitamin balance. Too much of one vitamin, as most parents recognize, will be spit out without delay. Just enough carrots will be eaten to achieve the required balance. In the same way, people in an organization need a proper balance of purposeful, objective-driven behavior and purposeless, freewheeling interaction, or else destructive conflicts will develop.

This is not to say that conflict must be counterproductive. In fact, conflicts, when properly controlled and resolved, can be a powerful tool for developing creative business plans and objectives. Without conflict, the organization would remain in a happy state of inactivity. However, to put this concept to use for the benefit of an organization, we must understand what enables people to interact in such a way as to make creative conflict resolution possible, and we must appreciate the barriers that all too often prevent resolution of conflicts and sow hate instead of trust.

This requires a thorough understanding of communication and of the psychology of individuals and groups. We must learn to transmit our thoughts clearly and to listen to our colleagues so as to grasp the real meaning of what they're telling us. We must listen to nuances and be aware of the hidden meanings in our own messages.

It is often said that communicative skills cannot be learned: Either you are a good communicator, or you are not. I think this is wrong, and in this book I attempt to show how we can improve our communicative skills.

I believe that when we learn to manage the interpersonal aspects of management, *synergy* will result. The synergistic organization is characterized by a feeling of internal harmony, which enables people to work with a sense of fulfillment and to enjoy what they do. When a synergistic environment has been created, the organization will be better able to cope with the many changes confronting business today, and the energy required to achieve meaningful work will be significantly reduced.

The key prerequisites for synergy are trust, effective communication, rapid feedback, and creativity. One of the most important jobs of today's managers is to establish these ingredients. They must hire people whom they can trust and create the conditions that make trust among the members of their group possible. Often this involves sharpening one's sensitivity to the hidden fears that prevent trust.

Managers must become good communicators and to a large extent control the extent and direction of communications in their domain of influence. Uncontrolled communication can result in understimulation, which stifles creativity, or in overstimulation, which can only result in confusion.

Managers must also become efficient in techniques of rapid feedback (nonverbal communication, including body language), both to encourage appropriate responses from colleagues and subordinates and to avoid undue interruptions in the flow of communication. Where communications slow down, the organization's ability to respond to changes is severely impaired.

Finally, managers must create the conditions for creativity. They must understand the mechanisms by which an individual arrives at creative solutions to a problem, and must learn to organize groups that can replicate such behavior. Creativity, as we will see in Chapter 4, is more likely to occur in a carefully selected group than in the individual; however, it is up to the manager to organize groups according to the nature of the problem at hand so as to maximize the chances for creative solutions.

None of this is easily achieved. There are many barriers to creating synergy, some of which may at times seem insuperable. However, I believe firmly that the techniques necessary to bring about synergy can be learned, and I hope that this book will be helpful in this important task.

Conflict
in the
Organization

2

Like the modern society in which it operates, the typical business organization of today is significantly more complex than its predecessors. It employs more people and must adjust to an accelerating rate of change. Specialists within the organization have become more sophisticated in their professionalism, and coordination of objectives and activities has become more difficult.

Top management still retains control of the organization finances, but as organizations have become multinational, multiproduct conglomerates, it has been necessary to divide them increasingly into subunits in order to facilitate planning and communications. There is decentralized authority, but financial control remains centralized.

Decentralized authority with centralized control represents a basic dichotomy, and it cannot be expanded indefinitely. Authority implies control, and the weaker the relationship between them, the more disorganized the organization will become. The organization of tomorrow will have still more specialists, there will be more divisions, people, and products, and the task of responding to change will become even more difficult than it is today.

With the accelerating rate of change, there is an increased need for the organization to plan on a short-term basis. Unless top management keeps track of short-range plans, it will have to relinquish all control. Since tight financial control will continue to be necessary, the increased emphasis on short-range plans means that we will need more sophisticated systems of communication within the organization.

This implies that the business of tomorrow will be organized differently. The organization of today is structured mainly to facilitate communications among people so that coordination can be achieved on a long-term basis; coordination of short-term activities was largely taken for granted. As short-term plans become important and more complex, communication within the groups responsible for formulating and implementing them must be given full attention.

In a way, business is built on conflict. Conflict, you might say, is the mother of change. You see a problem and do something to remove it. After it has been eliminated, conditions are no longer the same. Through change, the organization strengthens itself and restores harmony within itself and with its environment. As we will see, the modern organization of necessity creates a multitude of conflicts between individuals and groups and their different objectives, as well as between long-range and short-range plans. Although this is not bad in itself, we need to make sure that we have mechanisms for resolving such conflicts in a fruitful way. This can only be achieved by improving communications throughout the organization.

Problems are solved not by mandating rigorous management techniques, but by discussing them openly and in a positive frame of mind, by securing different views of them and integrating those views into a creative solution.

Before we discuss communication-based mechanisms of conflict resolution, however, let us take a brief look at the structure of the modern business organization and some of the approaches used in the past to reduce conflict.

Classical Features of the Organization

Business theorists generally see four characteristics as common to all organizations: (1) people directed toward an objective, (2) coordination of different activities, (3) a team organization, or groups of people, and (4) a system of decentralization, or a hierarchy. A closer look at each of these characteristics will give us a better understanding of why organizations tend to be relatively inflexible, what kinds of conflicts are likely to develop, and what it takes to resolve them.

The organization's objective

The concept of objectives is one of our most important. The nightmare of responsible people is having no objective to follow. Games, hobbies, and jobs are all techniques for establishing objectives, whether they be temporary or permanent. Objectives are essential for psychological balance. Even children exemplify the importance of objectives. Their objective is not to make trouble or noise as you might initially think, it may be to develop toward adulthood or gain experience. They may form an organization, give it a name, elect officers, collect dues, and make a meeting house, but the club breaks up as soon as they realize that they have nothing left to do.

In most organizations today, the objective that provides the unifying force and psychological and economic stability is to make a profit. This is not necessarily so; in many cases, the prime objective may be to fulfill a social need, cure a disease, eliminate pollution, or achieve some other well-defined goal.

Notice the immediate problem. The organization may have an objective that is in harmony with those of other organizations in the world, but this does little for the specialists who work within the organization. A profit objective or anti-pollution objective does little for the computer specialist laboring to develop a program for analyzing sales territories. In order for the objective to be of service to the computer specialist, it must relate to his or her personal job responsibility.

To specialists, the profit objective is so general that it provides little inspiration. To be effective, they must see a problem that they can solve through their own talents. The more closely allied the objective is to their specialty, the more profound their solution to the problem can be. If the objective is too far removed from the specialty, the number of ways in which it can be satisfied becomes large, and the work output of the specialist may be unrelated to the needs of the organization.

Modern organizations are aware of this problem, and they counter it by translating the single objective of the organization into a coordinated group of objectives for specialists. But it is precisely because of this splitting up of the primary objective into a number of subobjectives that the organization loses its ability to adapt to the changing environment.

As the organization increases in size and the number of employees and the degree of specialization grow, the task of specifying and coordinating subobjectives becomes accordingly more complex. You can sense that as the web of subobjectives grows, the ability of the group to change its course of action becomes proportionately limited. In essence, the subobjectives of other groups act as inertia, because any change in one set of subobjectives requires that other subobjectives are adjusted accordingly.

Inflexibility is linked not only to the number of objectives but also to the personal nature of some of the objectives and the conflict that grows from changing personal values. People elect—or are assigned—specific subobjectives not necessarily because of their training and background, but often because of their psychological makeup. This implies that some objectives may become unattainable by default: People will simply not accept them.

You can assume that every person in your company has personal objectives that are being satisfied by working in the organization. Just because the organization changes its direction does not mean that its employees will change their intentions or interests. They may have a burning desire to write a magazine article about their computer program and will not be happy to give up this project in order to begin working on another, unrelated task.

The existence of personal subobjectives can contribute to the organization's inflexibility and create serious conflicts between what the individual wants and what the organization wants. We have already acknowledged that conflict is good; however, if the discrepancy between objectives is too great, or if too many objectives are changed by mandate and without consideration of people's personal interests, the conflicts that develop might be beyond resolution, and individuals may be unable to adjust to the demands made on them.

It is futile to try to control conflicts caused by differences in objectives by a careful selection of people. At the best, this will work for a limited period of time. For one thing, the objectives of the people themselves are subject to unpredictable change. For another, we cannot hire new people each time the organization's objectives change, because there must be some continuity of employees. In general, the motivational chicanery whereby employees are fooled into thinking that their personal objectives will be fulfilled when organizational objectives are satisfied will not work indefinitely.

It's apparent, then, that some techniques of conflict resolution are needed. The organization must retain its ability to respond to change, and it must do so in spite of the many conflicts that are bound to arise.

Coordination of activities in the organization

The need for coordination, as we said, arises because the organization's general objective is split into a multitude of subobjectives for specialists. The problem is further complicated by the fact that each specialist must work on a series of objectives and has to establish a priority among them. Not only is it important that the specialists see the relative importance of their projects, it is also critical that they work on each project at the proper time. Consider the futility of developing a new product that is not manufactured until three years later. Where this happens, an important business opportunity may have been lost because of management's failure to properly coordinate research and manufacturing.

James Mooney thinks that coordination is the most important of all principles of business organization.[1] This makes sense insofar as the organization has available only limited resources. If it had overabundant manpower and capital, there would be little wrong, for instance, with development of a product three years prior to manufacturing; the only evil would be that the funds channeled into research and development could have more appropriately been used elsewhere or earned interest in a bank until such time when the development could be better coordinated with the organization's other needs.

The need for coordination has a significant impact on the organization's flexibility. Businesses must continuously adjust to changes in their markets and in society. However, any change that is made requires the coordinated modification of a host of different objectives, or else the organization's resources will not be used in the best way.

A conceivable way to achieve coordination of the different activities within the organization would be to relegate this critical task to outside coordination experts. However, the general consensus is that the coordination is seen as one of their prime responsibilities. They must see the whole operation, not just disjointed subobjectives, and guide it to specific ends. This is not always an easy task, and it is made no easier by the progressive division of the organization into groups and subunits, which adds to the complexity and inflexibility of the total structure.

Groups in the organization

The secret to understanding why the division of people into groups does nothing to lessen the organization's problems of adapting to change rests with understanding the role of the group leaders. They are responsible for coordinating activities within their groups, and, in cooperation with other group leaders, they must provide a general format into which the contributions of all the specialists within the group can be arranged.

The problem here is that any chain is only as strong as its weakest link. Where we have a number of group leaders, any one of them can destroy coordination and flexibility if he fails to coordinate his group with others.

Part of the inflexibility created by group leaders may be explained by considering the issue of specialization: Whereas the different group members are usually specialists, the group leader is typically someone between a specialist and generalist. Chances are excellent that he or she has difficulties understanding and appreciating the contributions of other groups. Without such an understanding, however, the group leader will not be effective at integrating the efforts of his or her group with those of others.

As a sidelight to our discussion of the group leader, we may have found a solution to the paradox of the Peter Principle.[2] The Peter Principle says that individuals will be promoted until they reach their point of inefficiency. If this theory were correct, most top executives should be incompetent, and the destruction of their companies should be but a matter of time.

Although it seems difficult to dispute the logic of this argument, many great companies, like General Motors or Bell Telephone, have flourished in blatant disregard of this ingenious theory. How can this be possible?

In the light of our discussion, the answer may be that people are promoted not because they're efficient specialists but because they are valuable as critical links in the hierarchical structure, thanks to their ability to transcend the specialist's point of view. Although perhaps quite inefficient as specialists, they may be effective leaders because they have developed the generalist's ability to reach a quick, albeit shallow, understanding of many different specialties.

The organizational hierarchy

Because the subgroups in the organization are composed of people, you must expect that the organization will be subjected to some of the pressures to which people themselves are exposed. More specifically, groups are sensitive to emotional factors. Therefore, organizations are strongly influenced by things such as the friendships that exist between people, and there is no reason to suspect that personal friendships are in harmony with positions in the hierarchy.

Wives, cultural interests, professional societies, and club associates all combine to increase the social stature of an individual beyond the limits specified in the organization chart. Because personal friendships exist at scattered places throughout the hierarchy, and because they tend to violate the formal principles of the organization, it is possible that a subordinate can in fact be regarded and treated as a superior.

A further complication in the organizational hierarchy is caused by the existence of "special employees." Often a company feels a special responsibility to such people, and they are kept long after they have lost their utility. They remain figureheads without function, filling a void in the hierarchical chart but serving little purpose. Consequently, they give rise to confusion.

One last, but no less important, way in which the organization's hierarchical structure may be upset is through the informal communication patterns that become established within the company. Some employees tend to act as communicators, passing on information as they receive it; others do not. The communicators may not always be the formally appointed leaders. For example, it is possible that a secretary can inform her boss of activities in the organization because she happens to be friends with another secretary who has access to key information.

This unofficial information transmittal network is known as the "grapevine." Its sources are many; it can originate from the secretary who has access to confidential information, from waste-baskets, thin walls, or even speculation. In a sense, it can be viewed as a response to the ineffectiveness of the official communication system, and it is baffling to observe how often this disorganized, unplanned system is strikingly more successful than the organization's formal information network.

The grapevine would be a valuable medium in a company if it could be relied upon to transmit information accurately. Usually, however, only gossip is transmitted reliably. It seems to be a basic human quality to pass on trivia. Other, important information typically is subject to uncontrollable distortion or is altogether not transmitted.

Because it is beyond the power of the company to control the flow of information through the grapevine, it cannot be used as a dependable communication system.

The upshot of all this is that the modern organization is more like a fuzzy ball than like a well-ordered group of people. When an opportunity for change occurs, the fuzzy ball may distort somewhat, but the appropriate response to changed conditions more often will be accidental than planned. People and responsibilities are either organized so tightly as to render the organization inflexible, or, conversely, so disorganized that adapting to change becomes equally impossible. Often, both these limitations can be found within the same organization. Because of these shortcomings, the most beneficial form of conflict resolution frequently is the least likely to occur.

Conflict Reduction Modes

The modern organization is rife with conflict. It starts with the need for two conflicting plans, one long-range and the other short-range. There is need for controlled stimulation in the midst of overstimulation, and for flexibility within an inflexible framework. In practice, there may be conflicts between research and development and engineering, engineering and manufacturing, manufacturing and production control.

This is good; there should be conflict. But it cannot persist. Yet there is a tendency for this to happen, because conflict reduction involves change, and the relative inflexibility of the organization resists such change. Let us take a brief look at some ways to resolve conflicts within the organization.

Breakdown

If a conflict remains unresolved, important opportunities may be lost. But this is not the only way in which conflict can prove to be damaging to a company. Conflicts may turn out to be costly in that they create disruptive emotions. Individuals involved in a persisting conflict are apt to feel frustration, and their behavior is likely to reflect this emotion. How many times have you been told to talk to some engineer or accountant who never understands what you are talking about? After a while, even the suggestion that you talk to the person turns your face red with anger.

One way to resolve such conflicts is *withdrawal*. You might simply stop talking to that person, or at least reduce communication to a minimum. Although it may reduce personal anxiety, this "breakdown" form of conflict reduction is of little use to the company because its economic, legal, or political environment does not change when people stop communicating.

Ironically, this form of conflict reduction seems the most common in the modern organization. Possibly because of the complexity of the organization, people feel the futility of trying to resolve conflicts and therefore save themselves anxiety by allowing breakdown to occur.

People not talking to each other, unanswered memos, avoidance of business issues, departments that just do not get along together—all these are examples of conflict reduction by breakdown. Unfortunately, this form of conflict reduction saves the self at the price of the organization. There are other modes of conflict reduction which, although requiring more effort, are far more beneficial to the organization.

Compromise

Once every year we formulate our five-year plan. This process takes two weeks, and it reminds me of taking finals during the senior year of college. After months of less serious effort, it is a brief period of intense concentration.

At one such occasion, I remember, a colleague needed my help. He too was writing his report, and he was harassed and frustrated as I was. Our boss wished to coordinate three reports into one book, and he wanted it to be well organized. This meant that my colleague and I had to trade information; in fact, we had to write sections for each other.

That afternoon, my colleague needed my R&D budget for one of the product categories for which I was responsible. I told him it would take a couple of days before I could get to it. Shortly thereafter, I needed a short write-up from my colleague on the strategy he was developing for cost reduction on precision optics. He too was busy and told me it would be a couple of days before he could get to it. In the end, we exchanged the relevant information within two hours.

In essence, we had compromised. He gave in a little and granted me a higher priority, and I did the same for him. This conflict reduction differs greatly from that in the preceding example. There is conflict reduction in a personal sense: We both remain good friends. We are anxious to help each other again, and we enjoy doing a good job for each other. There is also conflict reduction in a corporate sense: The organization needed integration of our written reports, and it achieved this end. We both changed our directions a little bit and thereby helped the group.

This kind of compromise is quite common in organization life. You have probably heard it formalized in terms like "You scratch my back, and I'll scratch yours." Each individual gives something up. The thing that is surrendered may be time that could have been spent writing a report or budgeting expenses, or it may be technical expertise. Every time a compromise occurs, there is a trade between values rendered and values received.

The lack of formality in compromise solutions has a positive effect, but it is somewhat risky. In the absence of formal procedures, people work by trust. There is no written contract or overt consequence of a lack of cooperation. If a compromise is made in good faith, trust is established, and this is of critical value between working associates because it makes more meaningful conflict reductions possible.

I said that this type of conflict resolution is risky. Clearly, if I had not "paid up" with the return of a written document shortly after I received my colleague's report, it would have been difficult to obtain a favor the next time. In fact, if one of us repeatedly failed to live up to expectation, breakdown would probably be quick to occur and we might withdraw from each other.

Compromise as exemplified in this case must represent a middle road. There is some instability in it, some waiting to see what the other person will do. In a sense, it involves some apathy: People must be willing to give up a little in order to get a little. They take a chance, and if they lose, so what?

Perhaps this is a harsh way to judge myself and my associate, but I think it is accurate. This is not to say that I believe that our *general* attitude was one of apathy, but only our attitude toward the reports we had to deliver. They were clearly not among the items that were highest on our lists of priorities, and we had little to lose by acceding to each other's demands.

Compromise is a valuable form of conflict reduction in cases where the outcome is relatively insignificant. However, it is a mistake to regard it as the best method, because in a compromise each party must sacrifice some of its goals, and there are many instances in which such a sacrifice is neither possible nor desirable. Because more ideal forms of conflict reduction require more energy, however, compromise may be recommended for minor conflicts.

Integration

A better form of conflict reduction would build attitudes that would prevent breakdown while fortifying the tendency to build trust. The optimum form of conflict reduction, well described by Mary Follet, is integration.[3] Integration on the corporate level is parallel to creativity on the individual level.

The first time I was ever aware of integration on an industrial level was when I was appointed to the position of marketing manager. I will always remember the occasion. At the time I was negotiating a sale. My company had invested several hundred thousand dollars in the development of a new optical polishing process. The process allowed us to produce glass plates that were flatter than those used in many industrial and commercial applications.

We saw a large market in our superflat glass, and we intended to market it in the office-copier field. We went to one of the giants in this field, and that company was indeed interested. Our newly developed ability was in line with its needs in two respects. First, its engineers needed glass that was flatter than conventionally provided, and second, because of the evolution of the new float glass processes, there was some speculation that plate glass would cease to be provided after a short time. It was imperative to our customer, however, to verify that our manufacturing process was a viable procedure capable of fulfilling its needs. In short, this customer wanted to see our process.

This presented a most interesting conflict. In order for the customer to buy, it was necessary for it to see a nonpatented process in which we had invested heavily. My upper management would not relent on this point, and the customer would not invest a nickel until it understood the nature of our process.

I invited the other purchasing agent to my office, and we discussed the problem. Each presented his point of view until the conflict was clearly visible. Then we went further. We talked about why we couldn't cooperate and what our fears were. I explained that we didn't want our costs known, and he expanded on certain engineering questions.

Suddenly, an idea appeared. It occurred to me that we could show the customer the room in which the process was performed. Its representatives could see the size of the room and the number of people working in it, and they could even initial the new stock on which we started the process. Although it was agreed that they would see the room, it was also agreed that the instruments in it would be cloaked with dark covers. We still laugh about it. The room was a mess, there were dark cloths over oil cans, and we raided the storage basement for other mysterious objects to cover.

In spite of the joke, this conflict was resolved through integration. The customer's representatives went out of the room, we closed the door, and 30 minutes later we came out with finished initialed products. We neither showed them our equipment nor disclosed the length of time required for the manufacturing process. The customer was satisfied that the process was viable and could be applied without an excessive number of people. In short, both our needs were satisfied, yet neither of us gave up anything essential. The customer wanted to be assured that the process was for real; I wanted the sale; my management wanted its secrecy. We all achieved our objectives through an integrated solution.

This solution required some creativity. A compromise, for in stance, might have required us to let the customer into the room and disclose some details of our process. This would have been appropriate if we had cared less about our objectives; however, in this case it was essential to us not to sacrifice our goals of secrecy.

The reason that I will always remember this occasion is that a strange bond developed between tthe customer's purchasing agent and myself. We suddenly became friends. There was a degree of mutual trust and cooperation that was unique in our companies. In past years, although we have moved away from this project, we have frequently consulted and achieved results on many other problems.

Integration requires conscientious work and creative thinking. Although it is our most desired type of thinking, it unfortunately is not commonplace in industry today.

A second example may help illustrate the concept of integration. Not too long ago, I was negotiating with a purchasing agent over the terms and conditions of a contract. There seemed to be general satisfaction with the price we had quoted, as well as with the fifteen or so general terms and conditions that we had identified as contingencies for our price. There was only one condition that precluded the closing of the sale, and this was being argued militantly by both myself and the buyer from the company with which I was negotiating.

The point under debate related to the scrap rate on the order. In this particular instance, we were chemically treating glassware that belonged to a customer. We quoted with the proviso that we would pay the customer in cash for glassware losses in excess of 5 percent. The customer, on the other hand, wanted us to treat each of several different product types individually and pay an excess on any single type where the excess was over 5 percent. Quite obviously, we preferred our proposal because it enabled us to average losses of over 5 percent in one category with lower losses in others. The customer did not want to yield on this point because its total accounting system was based on individual product types, and the averaging requested by us would have upset its accounting system.

In this case, there seemed to be a stalemate, for the customer was under pressure from its accounting group and dared not confuse the issue further. On the other hand, I had provided a fair price and was not willing to sacrifice further.

Suddenly an integrated solution was discovered. I suggested that if the other agent would credit my account for losses less than 5 percent on each product category, I would in turn credit his account for losses in excess of 5 percent. In this way, my customer would have a system that operated in accord with its accounting requirements, and I myself would be able to enjoy a bonus if our actual total loss was less than 5 percent.

As a result of our negotiation, we both enjoyed a system that significantly improved the terms and conditions under which we were working. As you may guess, my new-found friend and I were each quick to sign and close the deal.

What really happened in this process of integration? I believe that as we discussed the problem and our worries and needs, we began to define our objectives more accurately. When we started the negotiation, our objectives were very broad; then, in the course of our talks, we narrowed them down, and it became clear that we both had in fact started out with an inaccurate perception of our goals. Once we discovered our true objectives, the conflict, which heretofore seemed insuperable, could be resolved. Clearly, it required significant analysis to determine our real wants and needs in this arbitration process, but the investment paid off.

My last example of a conflict resolution pertained to a negotiation on an individual level. However, the organization as a whole faces an analogous task. When a change occurs in the evolution of a company—say, a shift in emphasis away from a major product line—this tends to create new conflicts among the many intertwined objectives of the organization. To restore the balance, a number of objectives may have to be redefined to eliminate the conflicts, and, in many cases, the solution hinges on a willingness to go back to the essentials and ask questions about the true goals of the organization or of particular subgroups.

Because of the number of people and the amount of work involved in such a process, it is tempting to adopt a passive attitude and let the majority of objectives persist in their well-established form. Where this happens, conflict becomes institutionalized, and the organization loses an opportunity to adapt to change.

We have seen, then, that the more productive forms of conflict resolution—namely compromise and integration—require either self-sacrifice or extra energy. It is for this reason that they do not normally occur. Business theorists, recognizing this fact, have generated techniques for overcoming the organization's natural barriers to conflict reduction. These techniques will be discussed in some detail in the following section. As we will see, these techniques achieve simplification of objectives in one way or another so as to reduce the creative energy required to resolve conflicts. In essence, these techniques try to overcome the shortcomings of the organization by a mechanical approach; therefore, I call these techniques "contrived control" systems. They tend to filter out a great number of objectives—many of them representing real needs—so as to provide focus on a few that may then be simplified to achieve a compromise or integration form of conflict reduction.

Contrived control has had many names, such as PERT or MBO, but they all have in common that they negate something from the system. The basic principle in synergistic management is that all the needs must be fully recognized; when this happens, the organization is optimally prepared to adapt to its environment. Mechanical simplification of objectives alone will not do.

Contrived Control

As we have seen in the last section, integration is the ideal form of conflict reduction. It blends together multiple needs, gives conflicting parties a sense of "winning," and, most important, provides a source of ideas and, thereby, a system for introducing change into the organization.

As has probably become clear, integration does not occur in everyday situations in corporate life. To a great extent, the ability to achieve integration depends on the degree of flexibility of the organization itself. Because of this, systems of contrived control are often used to facilitate the occurrence of integrative solutions.

Conflict reduction is a process by which change is introduced, and it is logical to expect that the drive for change will be pitted against a resistance to change. Contrived control is a class of techniques which have been introduced to overcome this natural resistance to change.

Because the nature of the organization has changed considerably in the evolution from a primitive business to a multinational multiproduct conglomerate, different forms of contrived control have been required during different industrial periods. In the following, these will be reviewed in more detail.

When we analyze contrived-control techniques used in the past, it appears that they were, above all, introduced to overcome the inflexibility caused by an improper number of stimuli within the organization. By stimuli, I simply mean any pieces of information, things you think about, things you hear, or problems that occur. In essence, they are the elemental concepts that cause people to think or an organization to be perturbed.

If there are too few or too many stimuli, the organization may be unable to function properly. For example, an organization adopting an excessive number of objectives can be confused to the point where nothing is achieved. On the other hand, if there is understimulation, the members of the organization may lack the input that they need in order to develop creative solutions to business problems.

Contrived control is a mechanism used to ensure the "right" amount of stimulation within the organization. What is "right" may of course vary from one organization to the other, depending on its stage of development and its general socioeconomic environment. The proper standard is difficult to establish, and moreover, it has changed throughout the history of management. Some of the most successful techniques include that of Gantt, the PERT system, MBO, Project Management, and Venture Management.[4] These will now be briefly reviewed, and I will suggest that none of them is likely to provide the correct stimulation balance. Without this balance, however, synergy, which we have recognized as an important goal in management, will not result.

The Gantt technique

The Gantt technique was invented by Henry Laurence Gantt (1861–1919), a contemporary of Frederick Taylor, who is recognized as the father of scientific management. Gantt's technique, developed for the U.S. government around 1917 and first used during World War I for the Emergency Fleet Corporation, was a revolutionary improvement over the planning and control systems of its time.

Its key tool is a visual chart on which future time is displayed horizontally and tasks to be completed are listed vertically. An example of such a chart is shown in Figure 1.

Obviously, there can be many variations and modifications of the chart. It is exemplified here as a planning chart, which is its prime use. All the tasks to be performed are listed, and the time required for completion of each is specified. Presumably, anyone looking at the chart can without difficulty determine the relative progress made on each subtask.

This technique fits well with the socioeconomic system of its time. In the period around 1920, management science was in its prime, and its focus was on production, wage incentives, and related issues. Problems of human relations, for instance, received little attention. If we were to characterize the management style of this period, we might call it Management by Force.

At this time, the war had come to an end, and there was an

Figure I. Typical example of a Gantt planning chart.

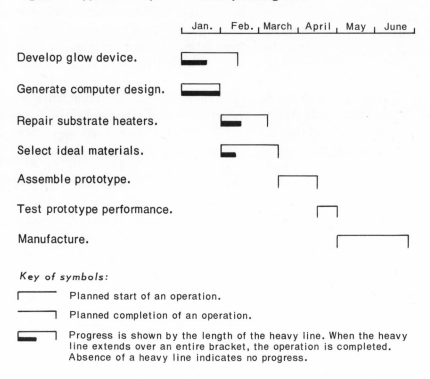

overabundance of workers and little legislation to protect their rights. Compared to today's standards, the rate of change was relatively slow, and the organization's need to respond to change was correspondingly less pressing than today.

The Gantt technique also reflected the functional needs of the organization at that time. The structure of the typical company was far less complex, and the need for coordination was therefore less critical. The leaders in the hierarchy were identified more clearly than is the case today.

Whereas today we view effective communications as perhaps *the* key to success, the concept then felt to be crucial for effective operation of the organization was that of objectives. As long as the people within the organization were aware of the objectives to be achieved, it was believed, profitable solutions to business problems were sure to be found. The brilliance of the Gantt technique is that it brings the organization's objectives to the attention of the working people, thereby providing the stimulation that is the prerequisite for developing creative solutions.

This relatively uncomplicated organization period was soon lost to the escalating rate of change and growing social reforms. Objectives were becoming more numerous and complex, and the need for coordination increasingly limited the organization's ability to adjust to change.

This can be confirmed by contrasting the economic situation of the 1920s with that of the early 1960s. The stage had been set by a series of influential events. The Great Depression posed new and difficult problems for business. In 1939, Roethlisberger and Dickson published their findings regarding the psychological motivation of workers and thereby changed the outlook on the people within the working ranks.[5] World War II and a rising inflation brought unprecedented challenges. Big unions, backed by stronger legislation, increasingly protected the rights of the worker.

As these changes took place, the Gantt planning technique was replaced by other systems.

PERT

PERT (Program Evaluation Review Technique), like the Gantt technique, was also introduced by the U.S. government. In 1958, the Special Project Office of the U.S. Navy, concerned with the execution of large military development programs, introduced it for its Polaris weapons system. Because of the inadequacy of the Gantt technique in providing better coordination in the light of increasingly more complex demands on business, it appears that a multitude of graphic techniques evolved between the 1940s and the 1960s, with PERT as the most popular.

Essential variations of PERT were the Line of Balance technique, introduced by Goodyear Tire and Rubber Company in 1941, and the Critical Path Method, developed in 1957 by E. I. du Pont de Nemours & Company. Both of these systems were aimed at facilitating coordination, but they differed in the amount of training required, the use of computers, and the areas for which they provide optimum control.

If one were to construct a PERT chart for the project shown in Figure 1, it would appear as shown in Figure 2. There are several points to be noted with regard to this chart. The chores to be completed are encircled, with the lines between the circles representing the amount of time that should be required to complete a given task. The numbers associated with each directional line denote the estimated completion time—in this case, weeks—for each task. Note that three numbers are given; they represent a pessimistic, an optimistic, and a most likely estimate.

The great advantage of this system is that it reflects more realistically the increased complexity of society and business, which makes exact time estimates impossible. The PERT system shows the relationships between the different tasks that must be accomplished. If one has to be completed before others can be started, this is clearly indicated.

Because the system is numerically based and focuses on the sequential order of tasks, it is easily adaptable to the computer, and most practitioners of PERT in fact make use of modern data processing aids, particularly if the total task is highly complex. Using the computer facilitates calculation of the completion time for the project and helps determine how to best allocate resources to minimize the time required.

In addition, because the different time values have been specified numerically, it is an easy matter to subject a program to statistical analyses and calculate the amount of variance that may be expected for the predicted values. The usefulness of this system becomes evident less in simple production tasks than in sophisticated planning problems.

Figure 2. Simplified PERT diagram for the plan shown in Figure I.

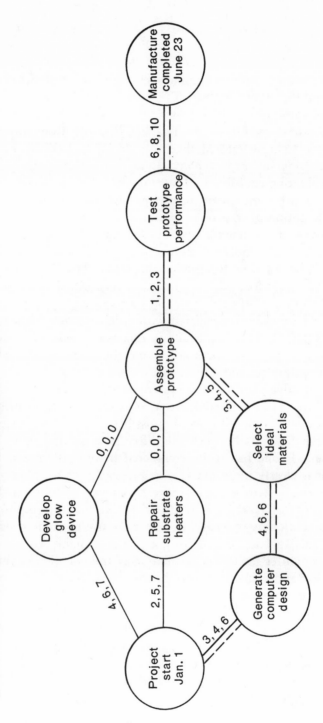

Key:
1. Solid lines indicate the number of weeks required to complete a task. Three numbers are given, representing an optimistic (first number), most likely (second number—corresponding to time shown on Gantt chart), and pessimistic (third number) estimate.
2. The broken line shows the *critical path* (activities that must be completed in the sequence and within the time limits shown). Tasks not on the critical path must be completed before the next task on the critical path is undertaken; within that limit, management can use discretion as to the exact scheduling of such tasks.

PERT fits well with many of the planning requirements of its period. In the 1960s, business was more complex than in the preceding decades, and the economy was expanding rapidly. Suddenly there were so many things in progress that it was difficult to maintain a concentrated effort on a single problem. There was, in effect, a situation of overstimulation.

You have undoubtedly noted the effects of overstimulation in your own work environment. In analyzing our divisional objectives this year, for instance, we noted that many of the things we were supposed to attend to had been neglected. It wasn't laziness. So many problems had accumulated over the year that to pay attention to all of them was impossible.

To solve this problem, we have created a new group this year whose specific task it is to control the activities that tend to disrupt our primary work. We believe that unless we do this, the problems will control us, instead of us controlling them.

The PERT system was designed as an aid in identifying and concentrating on the essential objectives of the organization. These objectives provide the basic stimuli without which the organization cannot function effectively. However, even in the economic environment of the 1960s, the objectives tended to be so numerous and complex that there was still overstimulation, raising the need for additional systems of coordination and control.

The number of groups within the typical organization had grown by 1960, and although the PERT system was helpful in indicating how they interacted, it largely ignored the increasing complexity of the hierarchy, which was a natural consequence of the progressive division of the organization into subunits.

In the early 1970s, PERT predictably began to lose popularity. As the hierarchical organization of corporations grew more and more complex and opaque, as it did in the decade from 1960 to 1970, it became crucial to restore the order within the hierarchy so as to ensure efficiency and proper coordination of activities. PERT became increasingly unable to meet this need. Yet other systems of contrived control seemed required.

Management by Objectives

The current formulations of MBO are credited to Peter Drucker,[6] who in 1964 suggested that managers should be held accountable for results. The principles of MBO were further developed by management practitioners who derived inspiration from the writings of Odiorne in 1965.[7] Today, knowing how to use this tool is a requirement of most managers.

MBO, sometimes referred to as Management by Results or Goals Management, has four defining features that are common to all its variants.[8] First, objectives are established for each position in the hierarchy. Most MBO systems require quantitative statements of objectives specifying what the manager is required to achieve and how much time he has to do it. In this way, progress on specific tasks can easily be measured. In this respect, MBO appears to be similar to both the Gantt and the PERT systems.

The next requirement in any MBO system is that objectives must be established jointly by the superior and his or her subordinates in an objective-setting session. Depending on the system used, the superior may set all the objectives with the subordinate in attendance, the subordinate may set all the objectives with the superior in attendance, or, in certain cases, an outside expert may be consulted in order to establish the objectives to be met by both superior and subordinate.

This second feature of MBO is new and distinguishes it from earlier systems. It acknowledges the importance of the hierarchy for the planning process in that different levels are now required to communicate about the objectives to be adopted.

The third aspect common to all MBO systems is that the objectives of one group must be linked to those of other groups. If sales, for instance, is projecting certain uses of inventory, this must be linked to production control's commitment to build inventory. This third aspect can be viewed as deriving from PERT's insistence on coordinating the efforts of different groups.

Finally, in all MBO systems there is an emphasis on measurement and control of the objectives that are selected. The underlying philosophy is that unless objectives are measured in some clear, unambiguous way, it will be impossible to control the progress made on them.

This feature implies the need for periodic reviews of objectives and for a mechanism allowing regular redrafting of objectives so that the system remains in phase with the progress achieved. This aspect of MBO, unlike the third, truly goes beyond the Gantt and PERT techniques. It recognizes the need to respond to change and provides a mechanical procedure for dealing with it. By contrast, the PERT system, for instance, allocates resources to fixed objectives, without taking into account the possible need for the objectives themselves to change.

It is instructive to examine the situations in which MBO, PERT, and the Gantt technique are most appropriately used. The Gantt technique was developed when *production* was the prime focus of industrial efforts. PERT was utilized when research and development became the key to success; it was less useful for production control systems. MBO can be used in many new ways, the most popular of which include improved corporate communication and control, quantification of the organization's goals, well-structured planning systems, a vehicle for team building, or a system of performance review.

Using the MBO system as a tool for planning involves two preliminary steps: a diagnosis and a prognosis. The diagnosis involves an evaluation of strengths and weaknesses. Strengths can include current share of market, technical expertise, or favorable economic condition. Weaknesses might include things like executive attitudes or poor product quality.

In the prognosis, the question to be answered is what will happen if no changes are made. In this step, it is assumed that the strengths and weaknesses will basically continue, with those factors controlled by the organization itself perhaps somewhat improved and those subject to interaction between the organization and its environment possibly becoming poorer.

The diagnosis and prognosis define the general situation to which the objectives must be adapted. Everybody involved in formulating objectives must be aware of these base conditions. In essence, if the prognosis is favorable, new objectives may not be required. Typically, however, the prognosis is somewhat less than rosy, and a number of changes and new objectives are required. These objectives are established in joint objective-setting sessions, as described earlier.

However, the MBO process is by no means complete with the formulation of objectives. After objectives are established on the divisional level, the group leaders return to their groups to formulate more specific sets of objectives. In this process, the objectives are more exactly defined, and it is here that most of the creative problem solving occurs. Specifically, at this point the strategies and tactics for implementing objectives are developed; that is, details of how, when, and where are settled.

In order to achieve utility from an MBO plan, it is essential to compare actual against planned progress on a periodic basis. In our company, this is done every quarter, which may in fact still be inadequate; however, it is all we can afford.

Reviewing objectives is a futile exercise unless it leads to change. Ideally the evaluation of progress against objectives should be fed back to the total hierarchy so that the prognosis can be revised as appropriate. If a new prognosis is generated, new objectives and subobjectives will naturally be formulated, and the flexibility of the organization is significantly improved.

Unfortunately, this works better in theory than in practice. For one thing, feedback presupposes that the information passed on in the form of quarterly reports and the like is processed in some depth. However, in real-life business situations, such reports are all too often skipped or not read at all, and this human factor reduces the value of the system considerably.

For another thing, performance reviews as demanded by MBO create a formidable amount of work, often more than can realistically be done on a quarterly basis. The upshot frequently is that reviews are done on an annual rather than a quarterly basis, which of course impairs the organization's ability to respond to changes.

As the rate of change accelerates, then, the MBO system will increasingly fail to meet real business needs, and new systems of contrived control that faciliate fast and effective communications will have to be developed.

Modern contrived control systems

Some of the larger corporations like 3M, Exxon, and Du Pont use a Venture Management technique. In general, it yields flexibility and some control of overstimulation. Venture Management calls for a separate, autonomous group whose task it is to introduce change. Once a budget for this group has been established, it is free to operate independently of other activities within the organization.

I created such a group within the confines of my own small division because I saw an important product line becoming obsolete, which ultimately would have meant the termination of a number of hitherto profitable operations.

There was, in this case, a clear need to change the organization's focus so as to forestall the predicted development; yet small disturbances continuously forced my group's attention away from the problems of introducing a major change. Establishing an independent effort appeared to be the only way to ensure the continuity of routine business while formulating plans for a total restructuring of our activities.

One critical factor that made it seem logical to establish such a Venture Group was that among my staff members was a uniquely creative individual who was regarded as a nomad by many of the people performing line functions in the organization. I realized that not only was this person eminently qualified to manage our venture project, but also the autonomy that would be granted him would free him of routine pressures and stimuli and thereby increase his effectiveness. After several discussions regarding the charter of our Venture Group, this individual was free to operate as he saw fit.

After operating this group for about nine months, an interesting problem developed. Within the nine-month period, a set of 10 to 12 patents had been disclosed, some working prototypes had been constructed, and the sales potentials and conservative forecasts were so much larger than our current levels of business that talk of this new effort assumed fairy-tale dimensions. Naturally, the company recognized our Venture Group as something of considerable value.

Because of the large sales projections, considerably more capital investment was required, and it was therefore felt necessary to integrate the venture effort more tightly into the greater organization structure. This was not an overt or purposeful reaction by higher management. Rather, as the organization's executives became concerned with the problem of obtaining the necessary capital, an increasing number of people automatically became involved with the project, and progress slowed as people debated about sums of money, added terms in contracts, legal advice, tax benefits, and the like.

This change of spirit of a Venture Management effort is perhaps typical of venture efforts. When the effort becomes valuable, it naturally receives more high-level attention, and attempts are made to control it and integrate it into the total organization. More often than not, this stifles the creativity of the group and decreases its efficiency.

Perhaps in response to this problem, some firms prefer Project Managers to Venture Groups. This approach differs from Venture Management mainly in that the Project Manager lacks the Venture Group's autonomy. Project Managers are staff members who are assigned to specific projects, and they must work with the line people to achieve their goals.

There is likely to develop a conflict between staff and line interests because the Project Manager imposes his needs where there may be limited resources to satisfy them. Typically, he must wrestle for performance from different departments, each of which has only limited time available and an overabundance of activities to attend to.

Because Project Managers are apt to create tension and conflict, their tenure tends to be limited. Even with great personal selling skills, they can usually achieve their ends only for a limited time because there is little they can give in return for the favors they must ask of others. In most cases, line people will soon tire of their interference and come to regard them as troublemakers.

In conclusion, it appears that these modern forms of contrived control are of limited value to the organization and unlikely to be used extensively in future management planning systems. There will be a need for new management systems that can cope more effectively with the problems of organizational inflexibility and overstimulation. The foremost professional requirements on future managers will be a thorough understanding of communications and the ability to control them.

Management by Communication

In formulating a modern contrived-control technique, it is essential to concentrate on the primary organization features—objectives, coordination, teams or groups, and the hierarchy. Each of these, I believe, must be simplified so that the organization's flexibility is restored and creative, productive resolution of conflicts becomes possible.

Because of the expected rate of change, it will also be necessary to somehow reduce the work associated with planning activities. The tedium normally associated with planning stems partly from the amount of paperwork involved, and partly from the mental attitude of people, and both of these factors can be adjusted once they are recognized. To illustrate this point with a simple example, consider the tedium involved in doing strenuous exercises: It can be alleviated by rhythmic breathing, thinking of something else, or merely telling oneself that it feels good. Similarly, tedium in planning can be reduced by working with associates who bring a positive attitude to the task and can divert the mind, but also by the success associated with your efforts.

I believe that the tedium of business life can be reduced, and the simplicity of the organization to some extent be restored, if we adopt a management style that might be called Management by Communication. Appropriately controlled communications can help us reduce paperwork to a minimum, cut across the hierarchy, speed up decisions, achieve continuity of planning, and replace frustration and mistrust by an atmosphere of harmony, trust, and cooperation.

The first item to consider is the formulation of objectives. Objectives should be developed in the effortless form of conversation, not only because this reduces the paperwork, but also because it speeds up the process and creates opportunities for rapid feedback and mutual stimulation.

At the same time, this way of handling objectives provides an excellent chance to improve communications across different levels of the hierarchy. I propose that beside the superior and the subordinate, two lower levels in the hierarchy be normally represented in the objective-setting sessions. First, this will introduce new and useful points of view, and second, it will contribute to creating a general spirit of cooperation.

Of course, the people from the lower levels of the hierarchy should be carefully selected. First, they must be relied upon to keep all information that is disclosed confidential because many of the planning activities are proprietary and crucial to the operations of the organization. The second criterion for selection is creativity. Developing objectives requires creativity, and blending different objectives presupposes an ability for integration.

The issue of integration of objectives perhaps sheds some light on the role of leaders in the hierarchy. Through proper selection of people and intelligent control of communications, these people must create the conditions for creative (in particular, "integrative") solutions to be formulated. They must make sure that there is neither overstimulation nor understimulation, for both are apt to create insuperable barriers to creativity.

One of the key problems faced by the leader is to restrict the number of objectives. Usually, when executives select objectives, they prepare a Christmas list: Everything that is desirable is on it. Objectives developed at this stage by an executive may number 15 to 20. Clearly, this represents overstimulation; with such a number of objectives, it is impossible to spend sufficient time on any particular one.

Whereas it requires limited creativity to generate a large number of objectives, reducing them to a sensible set of effective objectives does call for a high degree of creativity. Redundancies must be identified, and similar ideas must be combined to develop workable goals. In general, I feel that the total number of objectives for a group must be reduced, and this task clearly requires a formidable ability for integration on the part of the leader.

Another important reason why the number of objectives must be controlled is that this facilitates the task of coordination of different activities. But effective coordination depends not only on the number of objectives to be formulated and tracked for progress, but also on the attitude of people toward each other. Clearly, coordination is difficult to achieve if people are unwilling to cooperate and are insensitive to each other's needs.

No form of executive pressure can ensure a sense of commitment and cooperation among the members of the group. Rather, these qualities must be developed in a slow, purposeful process; and this is what this book is all about.

NOTES

1. Mooney, James D., *The Principles of Organization*, New York: Harper and Bros., 1947.
2. Peter, Laurence J., and Raymond Hull, *The Peter Principle*, New York: William Morrow, 1969.
3. Follet, Mary P., "Coordination," in Merill, H. F. (ed.), *Classics in Management*, New York: AMACOM, 1970.

4. The major portion of this survey of the history of management was derived from the original compilation of George S. Odiorne, *Management by Objectives*, New York: Pitman Publication Corporation, 1965.
5. Roethlisberger, Fritz J., and William J. Dickson, *Management and the Worker*, Cambridge, Mass.: Harvard University Press, 1939.
6. Drucker, Peter F., *Managing for Results*, New York: Harper & Row, 1964.
7. Odiorne, George S., *Management by Objectives*.
8. Reddin, William J., *Effective Management by Objectives*, New York: McGraw-Hill Book Company, 1971.

The Concept of Resonance

3

It was not long ago that I had the rare distinction of working with Dr. Charles Krandale. At the time, we were both working as physicists for a small company long since liquidated and burned to the ground. We knew the company would be liquidated; we could see the system which the principals had for stealing from each other. We were entranced by the way they used government funds to buy things from their own leasing company and changed the combination of the safe on each other.

Charles Krandale is a lifetime friend. We would talk for hours about what could be done to blow the whistle on the thieves, how we would like to break our contracts and be rid of the mess, or even what we would do with our lives after we were liberated from the strange situation in which we found ourselves.

We had a common problem: Neither of us was ready to go back to work. We had each spent $100 on 10,000 stocks and felt cheated with the realization that our stock was worthless. Nevertheless, we talked for hours about the feelings of entrepreneurship that we enjoyed.

Charles and I don't talk much anymore. He lives in Minneapolis, I in Rochester, and the price of our extended conversations is somewhat prohibitive. When we do talk, our conversations seem to go on and on without regard to the meter, which runs continuously, and we both find it difficult to terminate our discussions.

It is as though our conversation resonates. There is no tedium to our talk, no anxious thinking about what will be said next; the conversation seems to go on without labor.

If our energies had been properly channeled by the organization, it is possible that it would not have been liquidated. We might have continued to talk for endless hours about new ideas, which the company might have been able to use to its own benefit.

I don't know where the concept of resonance originated; I read about it in an old book that I finally located on a back shelf on the fourth floor at the University of Rochester library. The book was Richard LaPierre's *Collective Behaviour*, published in 1938.[1]

LaPierre noted the similarity between smiling in a conversation and singing in the bathtub. He theorized that people sing in the bathtub because they sound good. The sound of the voice is reinforced by both the bathroom tiles and the sound of falling water. Because the singer sounds good to himself, he is encouraged to sing louder and louder.

In the same way, a smile can enhance conversation. If a person is speaking and sees an interested face smiling back at him, he is encouraged to be funnier, louder, even more creative. The more encouragement he receives, the better he becomes. By sharing a smile, two people can enjoy a spontaneous conversation, whereas without it, there may be no real communication. The smile resonates a conversation just as the bathroom tiles resonate singing.

The term resonance is derived from the physical sciences. In this context, the term means "to amplify by sympathetic vibration." When two musical instruments, for example, play at the same frequency, they feed each other and thereby lessen the work involved in producing the sound. By this mechanism, a struck piano string can cause a piano string of a similar frequency to start vibrating as though it were struck. Analogously, two properly matched conversationalists can make each other talk so that a continuous, effortless dialog results.

Resonance does not happen automatically. The essential

prerequisites for it are effective communication, rapid feedback, trust, and a common code. One of the manager's most important tasks is to establish these conditions. When the proper foundation for resonance has been laid, conflict resolution, which we have earlier recognized as the key mechanism of change in the organization, will be that much easier to achieve. In the following, we will discuss these concepts in turn.

Communication

Clarence Browne defines communication as the process of transmitting ideas for the purpose of creating an understanding.[2] In still another definition, Ted McLaughlin et al. have defined communication as a mutual interchange of ideas by any effective means.[3] This latter definition acknowledges that people do not have singular roles of listener or speaker but are simultaneously both speakers and listeners.

For purposes of our discussion communication may be more narrowly defined as a mutual exchange of stimuli that gives rise to conflict resolution. For example, imagine a typical industrial setting where you want a raise and I want profitability. In our discussion, you might tell me that your family is having trouble making ends meet, that your child is ready for college, and so on. Perhaps you have three children attending college at the same time.

In exchange, I might tell you that the profitability of the division is down, that every $1,000 of additional expense results in our profit-to-sales ratio falling 0.1 percent, and so on.

The statements which we exchange are stimuli. As we talk about these things, you probably do not believe that the organization is doing as badly as I say it is, and in the end you might settle for a smaller raise than you initially asked for, and I might sacrifice a small percentage of the after-tax profits. I am satisfied since my key man is happy and my budget is not strained, and you are happy because you at least partly achieved what you wanted. Our final agreement reduces the conflict between our interests.

Communication, whether we realize this or not, is a purposeful process: People want to achieve something when they engage in a verbal exchange. They may want to persuade somebody, inform or be informed, or merely be entertained. More often than not, the goals of the communicators are not the same, even though a superficial look may make us believe that they are.

For example, we may communicate with the express purpose of exchanging ideas. At first sight our objectives seem to be the same. I may want to know what you know about a specific competitor, and you may want to know what I know about the same corporation. In truth, however, our objectives may be quite different: You want my information for a report you are writing, and I may want yours for a strategy that I am developing.

In order to achieve effective communication, each communicator must match his objective against those of the other persons involved in the exchange. To put it more simply, each communicator must know the objective of the people with whom he is communicating. Without such a common understanding, resonance and conflict resolution will be impossible.

Effective communication, then, involves more than talking and writing clearly. Listening skills are just as important as the ability to transmit your thoughts unambiguously. And listening does not stop at extracting the apparent message; you must also become sensitive to the clues that tell you about the sometimes not so apparent motives of the people talking to you. Often, this is possible only if you have appropriate background information about the speaker and are aware of his basic interests or even his philosophy of life.

You may consider it beyond your responsibility as a manager to take such an interest in the psychological makeup of your colleagues and subordinates, but I believe that unless you go to that trouble, true communication will be impossible, and resonance will remain an unattainable goal.

As we will see in later chapters, there are numerous ways to improve your skills both as a speaker and as a listener. Many of the most common barriers to communication can be overcome once you understand their nature and adjust your behavior so as to take their existence into account.

Some of these barriers are directly related to the communicative process and can be forestalled by using essentially mechanical techniques; others—which we may call "people barriers"—derive from deep-seated psychological attitudes and can be dealt with only if you understand what makes people behave the way they do.

In either case, your success as a synergistic manager crucially depends on your being sensitive to people, their needs and interests, and their strengths and weaknesses. Such sensitivity is not an innate, unchangeable quality. It can be learned, and furthermore, I believe that it is one of the prime responsibilities of today's managers to do their best to develop it in themselves and in others.

Rapid Feedback

Timely feedback is essential if resonance is to occur; without it, the communication process becomes slow, and tedium and frustration grow to the point where they endanger the success of any operation.

The importance of the concept of rapid feedback may be illustrated by returning to the analogy of the piano. I said earlier that if two piano strings are matched and close together, the striking of one string will cause the other to begin to vibrate. However, if one string is struck while the other is far removed, or if the second is brought in close proximity after the first has stopped vibrating, the second string will not vibrate.

Timing of feedback is equally important in communication. If a smile, for instance, occurs five minutes after the speaker has finished talking, he will derive little encouragement from it, and there is little opportunity for resonance.

It is imperative, then, that the time between stimulus and response be reduced to a minimum. In the extreme case, feedback may be simultaneous. Simultaneous feedback involves nods, smiles and frowns, and all those things that can be done without interrupting the flow of words. Unfortunately, the information that can be fed back in this way is of a rather limited nature, and consequently, most feedback must to some extent be separated in time from the original stimulus. However, the interval should generally not exceed thirty seconds.

There is nothing particularly sacred about this number. With a strong indication of interest on the part of the listener, the thirty seconds may in fact be extended by a factor of ten or more. However, I believe that under ordinary circumstances, talking for more than thirty seconds without any stimulus from the receiver greatly diminishes the chance of inducing resonance.

This points toward the futility of some common forms of communication. In Congress and at the United Nations, for instance, communication typically takes the form of thirty-minute speeches followed by thirty-minute replies. Here, the time that elapses between stimulus and response is so long that there is little chance to develop any resonance whatsoever.

Unfortunately, chances for resonance are even poorer in our modern industrial organizations. In business life, feedback, instead of being simultaneous, usually takes weeks or months, which makes for unnecessary tedium and in effect ensures that synergy will *not* result.

Typical of organization communications are five-minute presentations supported by visual displays and a written report, which the receiver is supposed to review after the verbal presentation is completed. In other cases, a written report alone may be sent for comment. With typical large-company mail service systems, the reply may come back two or three days after the message has been transmitted; in some cases, it may in fact never come back.

It appears, then, that the structure of the typical organization makes rapid feedback difficult to achieve. Decisions, for instance, usually involve the approval of superiors within the hierarchy. Approval of decisions is of course one of the most important types of feedback in a formal organization. As a result of the obligation to involve superiors, feedback is slowed. If approval must come from senior executives, the delay may be considerable, especially when all the information they require is initially not available.

This points to the importance of person-to-person interactions, which avoid the delays inherent in written communications, and of pre-agreed budgets and objectives, which cut down on the number of decisions needing higher-level approval. If these things are established vertically through the hierarchy, then much of the slow feedback which prevents resonance will be avoided.

Excessive emphasis on approval of decisions at upper levels of the hierarchy is an unfortunate feature of many management styles. Ideally, the limits of authority should be specified once according to a comprehensive plan, and reapproval should not be sought beyond the established limits. This thinking, however, seems to go against certain deeply ingrained principles of behavior. For some psychological reason, people feel that it is good to let their superiors know what they are doing and to obtain their approval of every activity.

There seems to be some confusion in this thinking. It is advisable to inform the boss about what you are doing so that he can appreciate your value to the organization; it is not advisable, however, to involve him in every decision of yours. Usually, the slowness of operations is caused by seeking unnecessary confirmation on preliminary decisions.

The reason that confirmation is sought is that there is a lack of trust. In general, because the superior does not trust the judgment of the subordinates, there is a need to check their decisions and reapprove their expenditure requests or requests for wages and so on. On the other hand, because they feel the lack of trust by the superior, subordinates spend a good deal of their efforts on telling the superior about their achievements and qualifications.

Trust within the organization is a critical ingredient that can relieve the need for inessential feedback. Without trust, communications are bound to become slow and ineffective.

Trust

Trust implies confidence, understanding, faith, and respect. Without it, resonance will be impossible, even if simultaneous feedback is present. You are unlikely to respond to the smile or laugh of someone for whom you have little or no respect.

We have seen, then, that there is a close association between trust and resonance. If trust exists, significantly less energy will be required to create resonance than would be possible by using rational arguments. I can talk to you until I am blue in the face about why you should trust me, and it will have little positive effect. Trust must be developed by developing emotions. How then can we build trust? Probably best by starting with ourselves and becoming trustworthy.

Gordon Lippitt points out that there are two kinds of trust: social trust and work trust.[4] He notes that social trust is prerequisite to work trust. Since work trust is essential to the functioning of the organization, it is necessary to begin by developing social trust.

Social trust is a reliance on integrity, or a feeling of confidence in a person as another human being. To establish social trust, a person must be judged on his or her inherent qualities. Clues in evaluating the social acceptability of people include family associations, attitudes toward value judgments, esthetic tastes, and so on.

When people first meet, they strive to develop this social trust. They talk about the weather, family associations, good restaurants, sources of recreation, hobbies, sports, homes—anything other than work. In summary, social trust implies confidence that an associate is proficient in the skill of living.

By contrast, work trust involves confidence in people's professional abilities. You can have work trust in a bricklayer who is good at laying bricks, a plumber who excels at soldering, an engineer who is proficient at calculating stress, or a manager with a silver tongue. This leaves room for imperfections: To establish work trust, it is not required that proficiency exist in all areas of professional activity, but only in some select area.

The responsibility for establishing trust must be shared between subordinate and superior. On one hand the manager must be able to rely on the subordinates to understand his or her weaknesses and to act in a responsible way in carrying out their duties. On the other hand, the subordinates must be able to show their feelings and act in a forthright manner without affecting the security of their job or the probability of promotion.

The process, as we have said, must start with the development of social trust. This calls for such apparently "trivial" things as talk about one's social life, the weather, and other topics unrelated to work. In such discussions the contributors are judging the social trustworthiness of their colleagues. More exactly, they are seeking areas of common feeling, which tend to build the strongest trust bonds.

In essence, then, the so-called trivial preliminary associations are not trivial at all; they are essential to the building of a base on which work trust can be established.

In a sense, establishing work trust is a simpler matter. The superior, for instance, may demonstrate an ability at analysis or organization that draws the respect of the subordinates. Similarly, the subordinate may exhibit proficiency in his speciality—be it organic chemistry or selling—that enables the superior to rely on his performance. When skill is shown, work trust can be established. Conversely, where there are doubts about people's proficiency in their specialty, it is difficult to establish work trust, no matter how secure social trust is.

As a manager who is interested in synergy, I have often considered it my duty to assist subordinates and associates in establishing trust within the organization environment. In this light, it has been my self-elected responsibility to push people together at times when social trust is lacking, and to discuss ways of improving professional skills when work trust is unsatisfactory.

This might require buying two people lunch or, more ideally, sending them out by themselves so that they may discover common feelings on which social trust can be built. When work trust is missing, it may be necessary to introduce group training sessions or other skill-building seminars.

It may seem beyond the responsibility of a conscientious manager to be involved with such things, but I feel that this is one of the most important tasks of the manager who is to be measured by his ability to construct a tightly knit group.

The Common Code

One important way to project work trust is through mastering the language of one's professional specialty. This is what we call the common code of a profession. It may be learned in college or on the job.

In order to see the relevance of a common code to resonance, consider the nature of a discussion that may take place through an interpreter. There is no direct contact between the two people involved with generating resonance. The words of each communicator must be chosen carefully in order to avoid ambiguity. In general, the mental focus is directed toward understanding rather than discovering and limiting objectives.

This type of situation can be contrasted with one where there is immediate understanding between the communicating parties. When this happens, the parties can without delay become involved in the sharing of ideas and in the discovery of common objectives, and the common code can be exploited for generating resonance.

It is both fortunate and unfortunate that the requirements of a common code are naturally satisfied in most corporate organizations. It is fortunate because the existence of a code removes this general barrier to effective communication and resonance. It is unfortunate because this accidental existence of a code in most industrial situations hides the importance of code from the management practitioner. When people take code for granted, they may be unable to establish it in those special cases where it is missing.

Fortunately, the grouping of people in the organization brings allied specialists closer together, and their interacting spheres of knowledge make the natural growth of a common work code possible. The juxtapositioning of scientists, for instance, whether they be physicists or chemists, allows for scientific talk and the enjoyment of code words common to both these specialties. Between widely divergent professional groups, the absence of code tends to create a barrier to resonance. In that sense, it is perhaps fortunate that there is relatively little interaction between these widely divergent groups.

The Conflict Resolution Process

Conflict, as we have seen, is not only unavoidable in any organization but also necessary for its well-being—provided it is resolved in a beneficial way. The ideal form of conflict resolution is "integration," which blends different objectives in such a way that no party must give up any of its essential goals. This distinguishes it from compromise solutions, in which each party must abandon some of its objectives.

Integration, unlike compromise or mere withdrawal, requires a high level of creativity. This is a worthwhile investment, however, for when integration occurs, it commonly goes along with a dramatic sense of achievement that can be a source for continued high-level productivity. By contrast, compromise resolutions of conflicts tend to be devoid of emotional titillation. For instance, when I agree to open a window half-way because you're cold and I'm warm, there is no excitement to be derived from this decision. I am giving in a little, and so are you; the matter is simply not worth fussing over.

It is important to appreciate this emotional aspect of integration. We have said earlier that creative conflict resolution, as exemplified by integration, is facilitated by resonance, or by a synergistic work environment. However, the uplifting emotion associated with integration in turn contributes to resonance. In a way, then, integration is both an effect and a cause of resonance.

Let me illustrate the process of conflict resolution with some examples drawn from my own experience.

A short while ago, one physicist in my research development and engineering group was complaining that the glass he was forced to use was causing a certain type of mirror that was made from it to have a very blurry quality. Consequently, he got in touch with the company's glass factory, which explained that it was aware of the problem and had approached several vendors and purchasing agents in order to buy improved materials.

In the meantime, our customer was notified of the problem and advised that operations would temporarily discontinue. There was a good degree of upset, because these mirrors were critically required by the customer for one of its products. Still, it seemed that nothing could be done about it.

Suddenly, it occurred to us that the imperfection could be removed by a polishing process. Quality Control was called in to consult, a few brief tests were made, the customer was notified of our intended solution, and within a few hours the shipment of the product resumed. Costs were slightly higher, but everyone was satisfied.

The conflict resolution in this case—namely the decision to polish the mirrors—was made possible by a properly balanced mix of stimuli in our group, and I believe that this balance in turn would have been difficult to achieve without resonance. As people discussed the problem, they talked about a great variety of things, and this served as a source of continuous stimulation, causing the minds of the people in the group to wander away from and back to the problem of concern.

In this process, stimuli mixed almost in a random process. Suddenly, and unpredictably, the right amount of stimuli mixed with the background knowledge of one creative individual and the solution was conceived. Interestingly enough, even though the crucial idea was due to a single individual, probably everyone thinks to this day that he suggested polishing the glass, and consequently all of us benefited spiritually from this achievement. This latter effect may be ascribed to the atmosphere of resonance and synergy, which, in a way, created the conditions necessary for the conception of the idea.

In another case, the delivery of a new product from our factory was being held up because the special measuring apparatus we needed was not delivered to us on schedule. As a result of this, our purchasing agent began to call the sales manager of the delinquent company and demand the promised delivery of the measuring equipment.

There seemed to be nothing that could be done, however. The measuring apparatus had not gone through the entire production cycle and consequently could not be shipped. This was most frustrating to my purchasing agent. He was authorized to approve overtime expense at our vendor's factory, but we were advised that this would do no good: Our vendor was in turn waiting for someone else.

After a number of further calls, we were told that the sales manager of this company could not be reached and the president and chairman of the board had been rushed to the hospital for an emergency. It was only after we asked in which hospital the president was resting that the sales manager agreed to discuss the problem with us in more depth.

It turned out that the real problem was that some of the parts still required a magnesium oxide overcoat to give the product a finished appearance. My purchasing agent was quick to indicate that he did not care what the product looked like as long as it worked, and so he authorized the delivery of the product without the overcoat. As a result, we could make our delivery, and our vendor company could sell its unfinished product at the price we had agreed to pay for the finished apparatus.

The conflict resolution in this second case hinged on the effective use of feedback. In essence, as we talked, each of us defined in progressively more detail the exact nature of our objectives. On first exposure, our objective was so broad that no matter what transpired, no solution seemed possible. As we talked with full openness and trust, we defined our objectives in enough detail so we could each see what the other wanted. After the objectives were narowed in this way, the solution to our problem became obvious. To come to an agreement, it was only necessary to realize that we each wanted different things.

This last case may not strike you as an example of a high-level conflict resolution. Nevertheless, it was a genuine instance of integration, and the people involved in the process derived a great deal of personal satisfaction from their achievement. In both cases,

I feel that resonance was generated as a result of a conflict resolution.

Feedback, as may have become clear from the last example, can play an important role in the resolution of conflicts. It increases the effectiveness of communication—in our example, by affording an opportunity to clarify the objectives of the different parties. At the same time, it contributes to resonance by providing additional stimuli that help people formulate new ideas.

Curiously enough, feedback may be useful even in cases where it contributes nothing to a more accurate transmission of messages. Occasionally, feedback may deepen misunderstandings rather than eliminate them, and under certain circumstances, the new angle introduced by the misunderstanding may lead to the conception of an idea that might otherwise not have come to the surface. Of course, if the misunderstanding is too great, it is unlikely that the different ideas will interact in any way; instead, there will simply be a deadlock.

An example showing how imperfect feedback can contribute to integration may help illustrate our point. There used to be a great deal of friction between a quality control group and an engineering group that I was directing. On one occasion, quality control was confronted with an inordinate number of rejects, so many that the group believed that its instrument was out of control. As a result of this, they consulted with the engineering group, which concluded that the optical system was out of alignment. Now to the quality control group, which lacked the necessary technical background, the only optical system it knew about was the light bulb. Consequently, quality control changed the light bulb, and by some fortunate coincidence, this turned out to be the solution to the problem.

Technically speaking, the feedback from engineering was not really helpful. It was mere chance that the light bulb had picked up a stain that was then projected to look as if it were on the final product. When engineering gave its advice, it obviously was thinking not about light bulbs but about rather sophisticated relationships between mechanical and optical parts. Because of the friction between the groups, quality control had been reluctant to ask for more help and simply did what it thought it had been instructed to do.

A pleasant and unexpected side effect of this affair was that quality control was grateful for the help it had received and returned to engineering to tell of the good results. Feedback was improved after this, and so was the relationship between the heretofore fending groups.

Conclusion

In this chapter, I have attempted to show that the organization's ability to resolve conflicts depends on establishing resonance, or "sympathetic vibrations." The most common barriers to resonance, as we have seen, are ineffective communications, slow or nonexistent feedback, and a lack of trust and code.

More than ever, organizations today must be flexible—that is, respond quickly to changes—and given the current rate of change, this is no easy task. Because of the complexity of today's business and society, the major problem in achieving or maintaining the required degree of flexibility is coordination of different activities and objectives, which typically are in conflict with one another.

It was our thesis that the coordination problem cannot be solved satisfactorily by mechanical procedures such as MBO; rather, these techniques must be supplemented by a management approach that recognizes the importance of communications and interpersonal relationships—in short, by a synergistic management style.

The manager's task, accordingly, is to create the conditions for resonance and synergy. This involves establishing a pattern of open, no-nonsense communication and rapid feedback, often cutting across well-established levels of the hierarchy. In this context, written communications should be minimized in favor of direct person-to-person communication.

To establish an atmosphere of trust, which we have recognized as another prerequisite of resonance, managers should encourage their subordinates to get to know one another on a social basis, and they must behave in such a way as to enable people to act in a forthright manner without fears for their positions or careers. At the same time, they may have to develop a willingness to trust their subordinates. Where there are genuine reasons for doubt in the professional skills of subordinates, the manager may have to insist on additional skill-building training sessions, unpopular as such a move may seem.

Finally, managers must make sure that the people in their groups share a common code, without which resonance will be difficult to achieve. Ordinarily, this requirement will be met because people have been exposed to and trained in the language of their profession before joining the organization. Occasionally, however, a code must be built from scratch, and managers must remain sensitive to this potential problem.

When all these conditions are satisfied, resonance will become a real possibility, and the organization's flexibility will be substantially improved. The work involved may be formidable, but I believe it will pay off.

NOTES

1. LaPierre, Richard T., *Collective Behavior*, New York: McGraw-Hill, 1938.
2. Browne, Clarence G., "Communication Means Understanding," in Keith Davis and William G. Scott (eds.), *Readings in Human Behavior*, New York: McGraw-Hill, 1959.
3. McLaughlin, Ted J., Lawrence P. Blum, and David M. Robinson, *Communication*, Columbus, Ohio: C. E. Merrill Books, 1964.
4. Lippitt, Gordon L., *Organization Renewal*, New York: Appleton-Century-Crofts, 1969.

Creativity
and
Synergy

4

There are two points that I would like to make crystal clear in this chapter. First, creativity, which is the basis of resonance, occurs more readily in a group than in the individual, and second, the emotions that feed resonance stem from creativity. When a group is working creatively, its emotional output is high, and the chances are excellent that synergistic management is at work, especially if prerequisites of simultaneous feedback, trust, and code are present. If they aren't, the group may fall into disarray.

The achievement of group creativity can transform such disarray into the synergistic management format. For example, when many researchers are working on individual projects, each researcher is of necessity immersed in his own problems. The trick is to assign several researchers to develop the same project. Under these conditions, several minds are concentrated on the same problem, and if success is achieved, the group will be further united through enjoyment of a common sense of satisfaction.

The manager's task in making this a fait accompli is actually easier than it seems. In the preceding chapter's discussion of creativity, it was noted that creativity in an organization is not the sole province of the researcher, but rather a benefit that should be derived from each and every member of the organization. Ordinary people working in groups can often develop ideas more easily than the lone inventor.

In the process of creativity people help each other with their varied ideas and seemingly disorganized thinking. When creativity actually occurs in this way, the group enjoys a powerful emotional uplift that is particularly gratifying to those involved. This emotional uplift tends to reduce the perceived amount of labor devoted to the work at hand, and thus motivates the organization's members to strive for higher standards of performance.

Creativity can be a normal outcome of group activity, particularly when the group is specially structured for this purpose and follows such well-documented procedures as "brainstorming." Perhaps a review of brainstorming will give the reader a more intuitive feeling for some of the fine points involved in creating resonance. Brainstorming's ground rules were formalized in 1953 when Alex Osborn wrote about the principles and procedures used to stimulate creative thinking by a group.[1]

Brainstorming is a contrived technique for generating ideas that eliminates some of the obstacles which inhibit individual creativity. Ordinarily, the mind is incapable of mixing mental images in a random way, but in the brainstorming situation, it is assisted in this mixing process by the cooperation of many minds, all generating ideas about the same topic.

Under conventional brainstorming technique, the active attention of a group is focused on a problem to develop new solutions. Osborn specified many rules to encourage participation by all members of the group and ensure a constant flow of new ideas. However, when the rules proposed by him and others are analyzed, one rule seems common to all: critical judgment must not be exercised, because it inhibits individual participation and changes the kind of thinking required by the group. The exercise of critical judgment forces the group to concentrate on specific points and analyze them, a process which inhibits creative thinking, because it destroys the freewheeling, "anything goes" atmosphere of the brainstorming session.

Because brainstorming works by building a fantasy environment that stimulates new ideas, it may be theorized that the group is an asset in this kind of activity because of its ability to develop a mental image of any hypothetical situation much more effectively than an individual. The group can add color and detail so that what is really a fantasy seems more lifelike and believable.

It is an easy matter to arrange a brainstorming session and see this power to project fantasy grow with the size of the group. Begin by asking the group to consider a statement such as: "Let's imagine a perfect convenience." Every member of the group must contribute to the idea rather than criticize any part of it. After a while the ideas start to flow: "How about a system where people fly up to the planes rather than have the planes land?" "Everyone can wear a Buck Rogers Jet Suit." "There can be a moving ramp on the back of the plane to lessen the problem of acceleration and deceleration." "There can be in-flight fueling." "A landing platform on the top of every house." As more and more people try to add to the central theme, more details are provided, and the imaginations of all those involved are stimulated to produce ever richer fantasies.

When critical judgment is not required, the mind functions on a lower level of consciousness, and it is while in this state that the chances of generating new ideas are optimized. However, it is difficult to control the exact level of consciousness required for creativity. For many reasons, we fluctuate between different levels of consciousness, and the exact mechanisms underlying this phenomenon are only imperfectly understood. States of concentration can be contrasted with states of daydreaming, sleep, or deep relaxation. In fact, it may be concluded that even within each of these activities there are levels of consciousness; for example, deep relaxation vs. relaxation. When one is hypnotized, he wakes immediately when it is suggested that he do something he would not normally do. On the other hand, there are bodily functions, such as pulse rate, which are mentally controlled but which cannot be consciously altered by the great majority of people.

It can be inferred that there is a continuum of states of consciousness ranging from the fully conscious to the unconscious. In the fully conscious state there is control of all mental signals, but as the mind moves into the less conscious states, there is less control and often daydreaming. It is in the latter mental state that stimuli readily enter the mind in a random manner, and it is almost a matter of chance as to how many can occur at one time.

In order to create you must avoid the more conscious mental

states, which means that you must put yourself in the mood for daydreaming and not exercise your critical judgment.

The rule of restricted negativism is usually complemented by other rules in brainstorming, depending on the author. Some typical additional rules include having an insufficient number of chairs for all of the people in the group, or presetting the duration of the meeting. The general assumption underlying this type of rule seems to be that artificially adding stress to a situation may contribute to changing people's normal thought patterns, thereby inducing them to develop innovative ideas.

Frequently, partial escape from consciousness can be achieved through the tutelage of a trained leader. Alternatively, procedures may be established that help the participants escape from their world of conscious concern.

One of the most interesting of the leader-oriented brainstorming techniques is that developed by William Gordon.[2] He states that creativity can be induced by a process (the synectic process) which involves (1) making the strange familiar; and (2) making the familiar strange. Step one includes identifying the problem and collecting all information associated with it. After this information base is fully absorbed by the group, the next step is to make the familiar strange. This is the stage where negativism is not allowed and where the generation of stimuli is required. The leader's role in this activity is to encourage the group to transfer its attention away from conscious problem solving.

Gordon's idea of viewing creativity as a two-stage process makes sense, because .it accommodates the natural stages associated with the generation of an idea. Academic specialists in creativity usually identify five stages involved in the development of an idea: recognition of a problem, collection of information, an incubation period, birth of the idea (illumination), and finally protection of the idea. Each stage must be satisfied in the creative process, and the chances of succeeding in this are much greater when a group rather than an individual is involved.

The Creative Process

Problem recognition is the first step of the creative process; however, it should not be regarded as a simple operation merely because it is first. You might consider a situation for a long time without recognizing the nature of the problem that is responsible for a particular situation. For example, you can study an unprofitable organization for a long time and still not know the nature of its problem. However, identify that problem as being in marketing and you can solve it.

Usually, it is easier to accomplish the first step of problem recognition when a group rather than an individual is involved. There are two reasons for this. First, when several people are involved in diagnosing a problem, some limited debate usually results about the source of the real problem. These differing views prevent fixation on any single symptom and limit the possibility that the real problem will be overlooked.

The second reason why group problem recognition is easier is that two people may actually be the cause of the problem, and when their personal interests are at stake, they can see it. The two have different conflict perspectives, and if their perspectives differ enough the problem becomes obvious.

The act of communication contributes significantly to the ease with which a problem is recognized. Problem recognition is facilitated by "talking it out." Frequently, a problem exists primarily within the subconscious. You feel that something is wrong. By talking out the problem, the mind's tendency to ramble on in the subconscious is thwarted, and hazy mental images are translated into precise words and logical word sequences. Conversation is a source of mutual motivation; statements stimulate other thoughts, questions lead to other questions, and eventually a better understanding of the real problem results.

After the problem is identified, the next stage involves the collection of information. To the creative individual, this usually means studying the data so that the required information is absorbed. With a group, such study is less tedious because the chore of assimilating knowledge can be divided among group members.

Each group member can teach his or her associates, and there is opportunity for asking questions, debating answers, and so on. When a group has special expertise, it is considerably easier to ask them a question and get an answer than it is to go to the library and search a dozen books until you find the answer you need.

Thus, for a variety of reasons, the collection of information is a significantly easier chore for a group than for an individual.

The advantages of the group that applied to the information

gathering chore apply as well to the incubation process. Incubation is a waiting process; waiting for an egg to hatch, or as in our case, waiting for an idea to be born. During the incubation period the environment must be carefully controlled; either mother hen sits on the egg or the egg is in a temperature-controlled chamber.

Conditions in the creative mind must also be carefully controlled if an idea is to hatch. The incubation process is not fully understood, but most authorities on the subject agree that the ideal mental environment for incubation consists of periods of deep concentration mixed with periods of total relaxation. Such an approach acknowledges that both the conscious mind and the subconscious mind contribute to the birth of a creative idea.

During the incubation period you let your conscious mind relax and let ideas stew within your subconscious mind. This process of stress and relaxation is pursued until an idea develops. When the mind is primed with a problem and the relevant background information, the incubation period starts, but minutes, months, or years may pass before the idea strikes.

In the incubation process, maintaining a balance between concentration and relaxation is critical, and only a few gifted minds can achieve this. Incubation in a group does not demand the same level of skill or seemingly neurotic behavior that may be required from an individual. In a group, members' contributions can be used to divert conscious attention away from the problem under study so that the subconscious minds of all the people involved can have an opportunity to work on the problem. In this regard, jokes or anecdotes told by one member tend to relax the group as a whole, and often the social pressure exerted by a peer's question does more to promote concentration than would self-discipline.

Undoubtedly, the most important aspect of simplifying the incubation process is analyzing the mental processes that occur. Incubation involves both conscious and subconscious thinking. Subconscious thought can be simulated by communication processes. In many ways, the communication approach is more efficient than the individual subconscious approach, and it is easy to note the failures of the subconscious technique that can be circumvented by communication.

As you daydream, your mind fixes on subjects, then jumps to unrelated subjects; hence it is difficult to control this kind of thinking. But the creative person tends to favor it, because the images come and go at a much faster rate than would be possible in conversation. Since these images appear and disappear rapidly and are often unrelated, some sort of filtering process is required. Therefore, those who are adept at such screening tend to favor the subconscious; but this choice involves a tradeoff: some degree of control for speed.

Communication may be used as a substitute for the random thinking activities of the subconscious. The conscious mind translates mental images from the near-subconscious into words. In essence, then, if you choose communication you must rely on the conscious mind and its ability to use deductive logic.

When the idea is born, the group's advantage over the individual lessens. Logic dictates that the final development of an idea should occur within a single mind; it is highly unlikely that the same solution would originate in two minds at the same instant. In spite of this, if you ask a group of people in a brainstorming session where an idea came from, each will often think that he was a significant contributor. It's a little like the situation in industry where when you ask a group of people how much they contributed to a successful product, the total is over 200 percent, as contrasted with a total of less than 100 percent when the subject is an unsuccessful product.

More important than the contribution of the group in the conceptualization of the actual idea is its contribution in preserving the idea after birth. The idea must move out of the mind of the inventor, otherwise he has no emotional outlet. A new idea must be tested against two acceptance standards. First, the idea is subject to experimental testing; that is, it must be established whether it works. Furthermore, the inventor must ask himself whether his invention provides the kind of benefits that have been predicted. Second, and equally important to the technical verification of an invention, is the academic acceptance. It is essential that the invention be accepted by the inventor's colleagues.

Frequently rejection occurs; colleagues may be jealous of the idea, or they may regard it as obvious and ignore it. The inventor thus must maintain support for his idea until it is accepted and protect it from attack, whatever the source.

The group can be particularly helpful in protecting the invention after it has been conceived during the process of finding practical applications. The different specialities available within the group make development of the idea a much more efficient process than would be the case if an individual were involved. Moreover, the group can provide social encouragement for the activity and thus remove some of the loneliness from the process of inventing. Unlike the individual who often must struggle to overcome preconceived negativism, the group can be mutually supportive and thus be free to engage in positive thinking.

In summary, the techniques that have been developed for brainstorming are interesting because they help the group establish an environment in which creativity can occur. Although we normally think of creativity as an individual process, it has been shown that, given the proper stimulation, an idea can originate within a group.

To gain more insight into the way in which a group simulates the creativity of an individual, it helps to note the predominant personality characteristics of a creative person and examine the situations in which these characteristics are copied by a group. In fact, as the modus operandi of the creative person is better understood, it becomes clear that he is motivated by his emotions. It is a justifiable extrapolation, then, to assume that the group is motivated by similar emotions. As this group emotion is amplified in concert with simultaneous feedback, code, and trust, synergistic management results.

The Creative Individual

Creative individuals tend to develop habits which contribute to the development of ideas. Because they seek conditions that may lead to creative stimulation, the creative develop personality quirks that distinguish them from the less creative people in our society. Often, these personality quirks give the creative individual a less than glamorous personality profile.

Because of this stereotype, the creative have been viewed as unorthodox. Thus the creative individual tends to disregard his public image, because he knows that by following those habits that result in creativity, he becomes more creative and reaps the ensuing rewards. It is not surprising, then, that the historian Elting Morison, when describing some thirty 19th-century inventors who flourished, commented that "a surprising number turned out to be people with little formal education, who drank a good deal, who were careless with money, and who had trouble with wives or other women."[3]

You might characterize the creative according to Morison's generalization. Or more specifically, you could speak of the creative person as being an introvert; you might look down on him as being out of step with society, and you might regard him as stubborn, curious, and persistent because of his endless hours of work in the laboratory. You might think of him as being super-industrious, very brilliant, somewhat disorderly, and very sloppy. In short, the general impression of the creative person is that of an eccentric who does not fit in with ordinary society.

Apart from your subjective view of creative people, there is experimental evidence that objectively defines the personality profile of the creative individual. Several studies correlate creative people (those who have demonstrated creativity by obtaining patents) with specific responses to sets of questions. It has been established that persistence, introversion, disorganization, and unusual mental balance are all measurable characteristics of the creative individual. As each of these characteristics is described, I will show how the group can replicate these individual personality traits; for example, the creative individual is introverted, and it will be explained how a group is often introverted, despite the apparent contradiction in terms.

Introversive behavior in the creative person

As an introvert, the creative person tends to ignore the social environment in which he lives, thereby reinforcing others' impression of him as an introvert. There are three major reasons why a creative person might tend to behave in this way. As an agent of change, the creative person may find little to talk about in the social setting in which he moves. Essentially, his problem is one of finding areas of common interest with the rest of society. Those areas which give society confidence and comfort are precisely the areas that the creative individual might be interested in changing. He cannot listen attentively to others because he has little interest in the subjects being discussed, and others cannot listen to him because they are equally disinterested.

Part of the creative person's inability to have two-way communication with others can be traced to his relative disinterest in people. The majority of creative people must be thing-oriented, at least those who work in industry. They tend to develop ideas in the physical sciences and deal with mechanical entities or even group concepts. Because they are conceptualizers, they have difficulty relating to the individual psyches of people within the organization. Their disinterest in people, coupled with a compensating interest in things, lays the foundation of a social barrier that not even the most conscientious efforts can remove.

The inability to become more socially amenable stems basically from the kind of thinking performed by the creative person. He is an unconscious thinker, and as such, he has taught himself that he is better off not concentrating. As a creator, he knows that creative concepts grow from the mix of stimuli within his mind. As discussed before, he allows these stimuli within his mind to mix with his background experience so as to achieve a combination that is most conducive to the development of an idea.

In the process, he tends to encourage his mind to work in a less conscious state because he knows that he is more apt to fantasize in that state. And encouraged by past successes, the creative person persists in the special kind of thinking that his work demands and thereby is induced to disregard society.

Given the personality makeup of a typical creative worker, you might wonder how a group can behave in this manner. At first glance the idea of an introverted group seems contradictory. To understand the relationship between the group and the introvert, it is essential to view the group as a unit within general society, and then its relationship to the characteristics of the introvert becomes clear.

For example, observe a clique at a cocktail party; in many ways their performance as a group is similar to that of the introvert. They may stand in a circle, talk in hushed tones, turn their backs on the rest of the macroscopic group, and in this posture carry on an extensive, private conversation. I admit that when I am conversing in this manner I tend to resent the outsider who intrudes on my private conversation by asking a question or contributing to the discussion in any way. Of course, my resentment is not strong; it is almost subconscious, but still I know it is there.

Perhaps you too have experienced this emotion. Perhaps in approaching my clique or some other clique, you too have felt shut out. In essence, the performance of the clique parallels the behavior of an introvert. Individuals within the clique become thing-oriented; they are absorbed by the concept under discussion, and they ignore the existing social environment.

A group that has found some subject which it can explore in new dimensions is reluctant to share it with others. It may be that there is subliminal fear that by bringing in outsiders, the ideas being discussed will be subject to some judgment and the whole fantasy may be destroyed.

Probably most prone to destruction is the way in which conversation is carried on by the clique. They, too, tend to talk in a less disciplined way than they would if they were in a situation which demanded concentration. If subjected to analysis, the group's conversation would be diagnosed as subconscious. Group members pause when talking, subject themselves to stimuli that come from their subconscious, stop listening and start to think about what they will say next, look at the people outside of the group, and, as far as society at large is concerned, exhibit all the characteristics of the individual, creative introvert.

Disorganized behavior in the creative person

The fact that the creative person enjoys working in his subconscious should suggest that he is a disorganized type, so it is logical to predict that he will project a disorganized self-image. Indeed, one immediately thinks of the inventor living in a messy room or working at a messy desk with papers strewn about.

In addition to the disorganized paperwork, there is his personal disorganization—wearing a brown sock and a black sock, forgetting where he put his shoes, disregarding a color match between shirt and necktie, and even absentmindedly forgetting what he was talking about. The creative person's disorganized living environment reflects the way he naturally files information within his mind.

It is possible that these stereotypes are popular misconceptions, reflecting opinions about a general class that were formed by observing the social habits of a few. If you will permit me a generalization, though, I believe that every inventor has a disorganized part within his own mind.

If you picture the mind as a large storage area, it is likely that the creative mind will put things in unusual places, places that would be unexpected in an orderly filing system. But by doing this, he might discover new things while looking for old things; he might ensure that his stimuli are mixed in a more random pattern. Of course, this action would be subconscious, no more conscious than his habit of keeping a messy desk, if in truth he has one.

A second reason why the creative person is probably disorganized grows out of the thinking that he must use. He must argue both sides of an inner conversation without being inconvenienced by the need for logic; and this lack of logical ties suggests disorganized behavior.

Even a properly organized management group is somewhat disorganized in its behavior, and if the manager or the leader of the brainstorming group is aware of the value of disorganization, he might achieve more creativity than expected. The source of the group's disorganization can be found by observing and listening to people as they converse. Conversationalists each think and talk; they do not always listen. They tend to fill in with words the ideas which have been developed in their minds. They think and speak.

This thinking before speaking is the element that tends to reduce any organization that might otherwise exist, because thinking, as we have noted previously, allows some randomness to enter into the conversation and thereby tends to disorganize it. Even in the case of logical, deductive thinking, there is disorganization because even if only people are involved, it is probable that they will think differently. Consequently, differences of opinion will develop, and these will have to be reconciled by further discussion and thought.

To illustrate how this disorganization process might occur in an industrial situation, consider a discussion among a physicist, a chemist, and a manufacturing manager. The physicist would want to explain a series of technical observations in terms of physical phenomena, the chemist might try to explain the same observations in terms of chemical phenomena, and the manufacturing manager, in terms of the differences between people.

The conversation would not be divided into three orderly, distinct presentations made by the physicist, the chemist, and the manufacturing manager. Instead, it will move back and forth among these individuals as new ideas are generated by conversational stimuli. The movement from point to point produces the disorganizing effect of creativity. In theory, this natural disorganization in conversation substitutes for the disorganization that exists in the mind of an inventor as he moves from subject to subject. Again, a parallel exists between the group and the individual.

The important thing to remember is that a conversation can produce the kind of thinking essential to the creative process more easily than solitary rumination. Very few people can just put their minds in neutral, sit back, and react to random stimuli from the subconscious. Groups in conversation, however, can achieve some aspects of this randomness without the inconvenience of this special kind of thinking. All that is required is the ability to speak in a spirit of open trust and then enjoy the pleasures of simultaneous feedback.

Persistence in the creative person

Of course, a new idea does not automatically occur as soon as disorganized behavior and introversive thinking are mixed together. It requires some effort before the new idea occurs, seemingly by chance. In other words, in order to be successful at creative thinking, one must persist at conversation for some time, and it is this quality of persistence which characterizes the creative individual and the creative group.

Persistence in the creative individual is more obvious. He is noted for his energy and tenaciousness, and when smitten with the need to prove a point, he struggles on without concern for his own feelings of tiredness. Perhaps his persistence is more obvious after his idea has been formulated. Have you ever noticed that the originator of an idea often suggests that it be used for an application where it does not seem to fit and constantly stresses its value in this use?

The strange truth is that after a creative idea is conceived, its creator is cursed with the need to have his idea accepted, and sometimes persists in his quest to the total disregard of all social amenities. Some theories postulate that the creative person cannot generate new ideas until he has seen his old idea through to completion.

I remember well my own wife remarking "God help us" when I came home one day and said "I have a great idea." She knows only too well that conceiving the idea is just the beginning of a long, expensive, and frustrating ordeal during which she will see little of her totally absorbed husband until the project is complete.

She also knows that while working with the idea I will be filled with anxiety and sometimes be quite despondent until the idea is either successfully developed or abandoned.

This quality of persistence can also be seen in the performance of groups. Observe people in argument as they work at reducing some conflict that might exist. They may say the same thing over and over; they may shout louder and louder in the hope of being heard; and they may try different combinations of logic to convince others and bring them around to their way of thinking. If you tell them that you understand, they generally keep on talking and tell you again anyhow. These aspects of persistence that exist in conversation substitute for the commitment to persistence that exists in the mind of the individual inventor.

With regard to persistence, it can be assumed that there is less anxiety among the people in a group than there is in the individual. The group has a way to vent its emotions and rid itself of frustration, but this is not possible for the individual saddled with pent-up emotion. For this reason, it is significantly easier to live with creativity in a group than it is to deal with it in an individual.

The persistence noted in the behavior of the creative individual may appear at the outset to be in conflict with the disorganized moodiness associated with the personality profile of a creative person. In fact, however, there is no conflict, even though you may sense one because creativity is a source of change and persistence is resistance to change. The apparent contradiction may be explained if we consider that the impulse to change may be so strong that it must be offset by a resistance to change, which exists within the creative individual as persistence.

This implies the existence of a psychological balance within people that must be maintained. If persistence is the psychological answer to the need to change, then you may postulate that there is within the creative individual a tendency to balance out the disorganization that is characteristic of the creative mind; for example, by peculiar habits such as always brushing the teeth with eyes closed or making ten trips to the hamper each morning. By offsetting disorganization with persistent habits, the creative person maintains an inherently healthy psyche, and this balance is itself a well-recognized aspect of the creative personality.

Balance in the creative person

The concept of balance in the creative should not be considered particularly unusual, because balance exists in all personality types. This is well documented by Alvin Toffler, who points out that each of us tends to offset points of organization with points of disorganization.[4] For example, if our work requires that we move frequently (instablity), this may be offset by a tendency to keep familiar possessions, such as a worn but comfortable easy chair (stability). The same pattern of stability versus instability, of organization versus disorganization, exists in the creative person, but the system of balance is stronger because the creative person tends to extremes in his behavior.

The maintenance-of-balance concept is particularly helpful in understanding the behavior of a creative individual with regard to the way he tends to treat information itself. Known facts are cherished by the creative person, because he will ultimately execute change by reordering basic information within his own mind. The facts are studied from every perspective; in layman's jargon, he knows his stuff cold. The basic information from which creativity will result is known in detail, and the relationships between all the parts are well understood.

This treatment of information provides a sense of stability that can be offset by acts of instability. As the creative person explores his known facts and begins to question basic theorems, mix theorems in a random way, or purposely disregard specific information, he pits instability against stability, and the balance is retained.

Balance is also required by the group. Balance within the group means that if some members are prone to create change, other individuals must be prone to resist it. The impulse to change must be matched against an impulse to resist change. The creative group has a strong advantage over the individual because individual group members can be agents of either change or stability, and consequently, the sensitive balance that normally exists within an individual is not required of individual group members. To achieve group balance the manager must be careful in his initial selection of people, but after that the chore is complete.

The concept of balance within a group can also be observed in some of the secondary functions associated with creativity. For example, information known to many people provides a stable base against which the specialized information of an individual can be compared. The normal redundancy in conversation can also be regarded as a stability platform for comparison with something unique (unstable). Together, the many people who function within a group create an environment that lessens the strain of maintaining that balance which is critical to the creative process.

After considering the many ways in which the group contributes to the creative process, one must conclude that the chance for success in creativity is greater for the group than for the individual. Within a properly organized group, creativity is almost an automatic process that results from the sometimes instinctive qualities of people and does not require the personality quirks of the creative individual. With the creative group, it is easier to achieve randomness, to receive stimulation, to promote persistence and balance, to recognize or create problems, and to provide the encouraging feedback that is so essential for a creative exchange. It is probably for a combination of these many reasons that brainstorming has become such a well-established technique.

This whole analysis of group effort in creative thinking is based on the assumption that people in a group talk with the intent of creating. It was mentioned previously that the group seems to pursue creativity in an instinctive way, and considering that there are relatively few things that humans pursue instinctively, it is reasonable to ask why I think in this way about creativity. In short, I base this conclusion on my observation of a strong sense of emotion that exists within and about the creative process. It seems evident to me that human beings are instinctively driven to do those things that evoke pleasant emotions, and creative work seems to be one of them.

Now, there is a close parallel between the individual in the act of creating and the group involved in creativity. Emotion is also the main driving force of the group, but group activity provides several advantages, such as unparalleled cohesiveness among members and a lessening of the tedium associated with the work.

Emotion in the Creative Act

Emotion in the creative act has been discussed in an earlier chapter. It may take the form of a general sense of euphoria, jumping up and down for joy, singing, jubilant conversation, feeling good, and an urge to tell everyone, including the neighborhood dog. It is an important fact that the creative process is associated with emotional outbursts. Because these emotions are pleasant sensations, man is motivated to create again so that he can enjoy more of the same pleasant emotions.

Again, an understanding of this behavior can be gained by considering the emotions associated with love. Much in the same way as a boy courts a girl, the inventor courts his idea. Remember the hand-holding, the heart-in-mouth sensation, the feeling of softness, and all the other symptoms of puppy love. Well, the inventor feels the same way about conditions that might result in a new idea. He feels a sense of excitement. Almost instinctively he senses that something nice is going to happen, but as with puppy love, there is not even a hint of the activities to follow.

When puppy love strikes, the youth primps as he prepares himself so that the emotion he feels can somehow be increased. The equivalent action by the creative conceptualizer is study. It is a passionate period of study in which he investigates all the information associated with the problem of his concern. In this process, the energy with which he pursues his study is generally greater than that which would be expended on routine work.

Eventually, puppy love dies out for one reason or another, and sometimes the sensation of an idea is similarly lost; but both will recur. As we mature, our emotions are replaced by stronger emotions, perhaps true love. Eventually a climax is attained, which can only be summarized as a very strong emotion. In achieving this emotion, the person has pursued all the steps that were previously associated with milder emotions such as puppy love.

In the pursuit of an idea, it is probable that all the emotions and learning that feed the process will climax in the actual development of the idea. This is the point where emotion is strongest. It may be likened to the act of love or perhaps more fittingly to a mother's emotion when her baby is born after nine months of pregnancy.

The mother loves her child, pampers it, feeds it, protects it, helps it to develop. She wakes in the middle of the night at the slightest change in the child's breathing rhythm. This would not be normal behavior because of the work involved unless it were done in an environment filled with very strong emotions.

The inventor behaves with his "child" in much the same way as the mother, and his motivation is based on similar emotions. He protects the idea against the analytical attacks of his colleagues, he thinks about how the idea might be developed commercially, he adds new concepts to the idea to increase its utility, and he labors with great passion to verify its workability. The strong emotion associated with his invention is both a part of the idea and a product of it; consequently, emotion remains for future creativity. For a mother, the equivalent would be having additional children because of the emotion associated with the first. The creative person is similarly motivated and uses his remaining emotion to develop the second or third idea.

The group can also anticipate the emotion associated with creativity, and each of its members can be motivated to devote his energy to the idea and can share the group's collective emotion on an individual basis. As the idea develops, the group works harder, its emotion builds in a way that provides energy for still more work. The outcome of the process is that the group labors in an emotional state, unaware of the energy that is being expended. Thus emotion provides that group resonance which distinguishes synergistic management.

Emotion in Synergy

The emotion of creativity has a strong influence on the individual and makes him feel better. Problems arise only when there is a difference of objectives; for example, the wife may want to buy a new couch and talk to her husband, who may want to buy an old lathe and work in the cellar.

From a corporate perspective, the emotion of creativity is the ideal motivator; it is more powerful than money or such other approaches as KITA, carrot and stick, Theory Y, positive stroke, and so on. Anticipation of a creative opportunity drives the researcher to reorganize his whole lifestyle and work habits, and this phenomenon can be used by organizations of the future to master the problems of adapting to rapid change.

The same emotions felt by the individual are experienced by the group when all members feel that they have been involved in the creative process. The group works with increased energy to make the new invention practical. Group members who may have been at odds become united by a bond that exceeds those established by work or social trust. Under these conditions, people have strong empathy for their associates, and they band together because they make one another feel good.

There is a right and a wrong way for managers to use the emotional output of the creative process. Some managers persuade subordinates to think that they suggested a concept when they really did not. They may tell the subordinate, "About a week ago, you suggested . . .," or they may talk around a subject until the subordinate suggests what the superior had in mind all along.

Such manipulation can motivate the subordinate, but his subconscious mind will probably be suspicious, and resonance will not occur. It is far better to come out with a definite idea and talk with the subordinate about improving it. After he has really improved it there should be an opportunity to work together. Under these latter conditions trust has been developed, and resonance can occur.

In using the emotional output of creativity, there is a temporal effect that the manager should recognize. Strong emotions exist after conflict resolution has occurred, but it is unreasonable to assume that these emotions last forever. The duration of the emotion probably depends on the degree of trust and internal creative desire involved. I have seen instances where the emotion has lasted for weeks, as with the simple solution of a quality control problem, or for years, as in the case of a complex marketing problem.

Because the emotion eventually diminishes, you must assume that it decays at some rate and eventually falls to a residual level, which is higher or lower, depending on the number of conflict resolutions involved.

The well-knit group is held together by the residual emotion shared by its members. This residual emotion must not be continuous but should fluctuate. Without conflict, the emotion is rather subtle; but with conflict, and depending on the rapport between individuals, the emotion can increase. As the solution is reached, the emotional fervor builds to a climax, and as the invention is made practical, a high level of emotion persists.

There is a danger with this emotional cycle in that when the emotion is rapidly decreased, the organization is susceptible to internal subdivision through conflict. Consequently, it is a critical function of the manager to control the level of emotion that prevails within the organization.

The manager of an organization must recognize that his primary task is control of the cycles which lead to resonance. Emotion is a useful tool, and it is the manager's job to know how to use and control it. If he can, the rewards of synergistic management are his. However, the manager involved with synergy must realize that although the basic ingredients are simple, there are many pitfalls that can destroy it. The process has many subtle and complex components, the most important of which will be discussed in the following chapters.

NOTES

1. Osborn, Alex F., *Applied Imagination*, New York: Scribner, 1957.
2. Gordon, William J. J., *Synectics*, New York: Harper & Row, 1961.
3. Morison, Elting, as quoted in David Allison, *The R&D Game*, Cambridge, Mass: M.I.T. Press, 1969.
4. Toffler, Alvin, *Future Shock*, New York: Random House, 1970.

The Manager's Role in Synergy

5

The advantages of a synergistic management system are many, and it is time to explore how to go about organizing a system whereby they can be reaped.

In establishing a synergistic management system, your first concern should be to evaluate your organizational environment and realistically determine your chances of success. To attempt to create resonance from scratch can be an energy-consuming and hazardous enterprise requiring great care, moderation, and patience. Goodwill alone is usually not enough.

An example may illustrate my point. I once worked for a company that hired an exceptionally bright professional engineer. Not only did he know his subject very well, he also had a great ability to sell the concepts on which he was working. He seemed to be able to persuade just about everybody of the value of the work he was undertaking.

On my first exposure to him, I marveled at what he was doing, but I also worried about his being fired. At that time, my company was a very sleepy organization. The people did not seem committed to hard work and spent many hours each day in idle conversation; in fact, their creativity appeared to be expended on devising ways to minimize work. The engineer, who was not blind to this situation, decided to perform a work-sampling analysis. During the day, he would randomly observe people at work and decide whether they were busy with company work or noncompany activities. From this he was able to determine how many people were required to perform critical tasks and how many could be applied to work elsewhere.

In all probability, this man saw his effort as directed at creating a more efficient and synergistic work environment. He intended to organize people into new, more productive groups and make them enjoy their work more while letting them contribute in a way that was more beneficial to the organization. The people in the organization, however, viewed his contribution quite differently. They were distrustful of him. They enjoyed doing what they were doing and developed a strong distaste for his activities. Because of their resentment, they began circulating rumors about him and formed a union, making it known that he was the one who forced them toward this action. As a result, the engineer was fired.

The process of creating resonance where there is none to begin with can be hazardous, and the manager who is interested in developing this management style is therefore advised to act carefully, gradually, and with moderation.

Even when you find yourself in an environment that seems ready for synergistic management, you must take care that the mood remains proper. People's attitudes can change in time, or alternatively, the thinking of the organization itself can change. For example, you might tell your subordinates exactly what you are planning to do, and they might agree to participate. However, after a short time, they may still build resentment, be it because of changed conditions at work or in their personal lives. If you fail to perceive the signs of resentment, you will find yourself back in trouble.

The same kind of transition can occur within the organization itself. For example, you may be working in a young organization where innovation and experiments are encouraged. Under such conditions, you may be free—and even encouraged—to change your ideas and approaches as you see fit. However, as soon as the organization matures, it might desire more control, even resonance itself.

In either case, you should continually monitor the trends in your organization and the emotions of all the individuals associated directly or indirectly with your efforts at establishing resonance.

This warning is not to be taken lightly. You must keep in mind that just as the rewards of synergistic management can be extraordinary, so can the risks. After assessing your situation, you may well come to the conclusion that you cannot go all the way. Resonance builds in degrees, and managers who understand the total process with all its dangers have the best chances of success in their efforts. Before investing your energies into building a synergistic environment, then, you should be clear about what it involves.

Staffing for Synergy

The first step in developing a synergistic management system is to hire the right people. But who are the right people? I have had two experiences in my recent industrial life from which I gained some insights into this problem, and I would like to relate them to you.

In the first case, I needed to hire a marketing manager. I interviewed a multitude of people who were referred to me through an employment agency. Finding no ideal candidate, I placed an advertisement in *The Wall Street Journal* and was almost immediately inundated with more than forty resumés. That was an excellent result, and I was particularly impressed with the high quality of the potential candidates. However, as I read the resumés, I noted that it was difficult to separate out the exceptional from the average; they all read alike. Eventually, I developed a scoring system for each resumé. With this system, I could read each resumé, assign a score to it, perform a multiple regression analysis including age, salary, and score, and thereby select the ideal candidate for my interests.

I was elated with my hire and by what I learned through this exercise. According to my own system, which of course was geared to the specific needs of the position to be filled, MBA's and

Ph.D's received the same credit for education. Similarly, equal credit was given for two technical papers as for twenty papers, for one patent or five patents, for two promotions or five, and for sales of $100,000 or $1,000,000. In looking at the applicants, a balance of capabilities was most important to me, and I was quick to sense that my own strong impulse to excel was not a requirement in my evaluation system; it was neither a benefit nor a detriment. I discovered something that I sensed was critical to a synergistic management system: the importance of moderation. This is perhaps the key quality to look out for when staffing for synergy.

My second lesson was just as instructive although somewhat distressing. I had just been passed up for a promotion. I was clearly the most qualified candidate, having superior skills in all the required areas. In fact, I was all the more disappointed since I felt that the person who received the job was far less competent than I.

Shortly thereafter I sought help from a retired executive who had become a teacher and still knew much about the people and the situation at the company. He told me that I was passed over because I was not trusted. I had top-secret clearance, had never stolen a thing or told a lie in my life, and found this a bitter pill to swallow. He explained that the man who got the job had been a subordinate of the senior executive responsible for the hiring for almost 25 years, had been originally hired by him, and had shared the same office with him for a number of years. He went on to explain that when a senior executive hires a subordinate, he does not care so much what he can do as how reliable he appears to be.

This was a bad omen for me because I had not been hired by the senior executive and did not want to wait 25 years for the type of job for which I felt qualified. Nonetheless, the experience was valuable, for it taught me a great deal about the importance of trust. Clearly, when you remove excellence, something worthwhile must be left.

Naturally, my first reaction was to grow very cynical of the role of trust. In fact, I became suspicious of my own subordinates. I suddenly remembered having read that a man should not have the same subordinate for more than six years, and this was beginning to make sense to me. If the subordinates are reasonably intelligent, they should be able to learn what kinds of answers I require, and once they have learned to adjust their responses superficially to my preferences, they may in fact make it impossible for me to get an accurate picture of the real situation. For example, they might know that I am very concerned over production yield, insist on timely reports, and so on. By complying with my concerns in these areas, they may be able to direct my attention away from other problems over which I should keep control. Similarly, they might know that the best time to get me to sign my name is on a Thursday before teaching, or that I like argument. In essence, through long association they know my strengths and weaknesses, and because they have learned to manipulate me to a certain extent, I must depend on them to supply me with the information I need.

Once I got over my cynicism, I soon realized that the problem is not how long to keep your subordinates. The real issue is that managers must be able to trust the people who work for them—regardless of how long their association has lasted. In their hiring activity, they must select those people on whose honesty and loyalty they can depend.

As we have seen, trust is not achieved automatically; rather, it must be developed in stages, from social trust to work trust. This implies that a critical role of managers is to cultivate a spirit of trust among all those with whom they work. They must know how to develop trust at the beginning and how to maintain it at that point when people become aware of how to fool them.

Trust implies confidence and respect, and to command these, you must start at home—by remaining trustworthy yourself. But more than this: You must also know your people's attitudes, capabilities, and habits so that you can anticipate their performance. In plain words, this means that it is your responsibility to understand in detail the thinking of your subordinates. This requires you to expend significant efforts at maintaining a continuous dialog with your people.

The manager who is aware of the need to trust others greatly simplifies his job if he can focus on the specific areas in which the existence of trust has the greatest impact on the operations of the organization. Knowledge that the subordinate will be reliable in attendance, not involved in embezzlement, and perform to the best of his ability constitutes a basic trust that does not require much judgment on the part of the manager. If this type of trust doesn't exist, the employee is probably dismissed at the outset.

A more subtle but equally critical area in which trust must be developed is judgment. After a reasonable period of training, you must be able to rely on subordinates to judge situations accurately and to develop the right answers—not necessarily the ones that agree with your thinking but rather those that are correct. In a large organization, this takes two important forms: (1) trust that subordinates will communicate judgments through the organization hierarchy without distortions, and (2) trust that they will limit the stimuli to which they expose both you and their subordinates. As we have seen, proper control of communications is a prime requirement of the modern organization, and without trust, this will remain an impossible task.

Trust in Hierarchy Communications

Trust in hierarchy communications represents confidence that communications within the organization will progress as intended. If this condition is met, it will theoretically not matter how far down in the hierarchy people are buried, because they will be exposed to all the information they need and the outcome of their work will be communicated to everybody who is concerned with it. Trust in hierarchy communications, then, is concerned with the extent, the timing, and the direction of communications.

As a manager, you must rely on your subordinates to transmit your desires accurately and without distortion to other subordinates within the organization. Usually, when information is transmitted from one individual to another through the hierarchy, some details are omitted while others are added. It is safe to conclude, therefore, that the content of messages tends to change significantly as they pass from superior to subordinates. You must take steps to prevent this from happening.

The way in which information is transmitted through an organization has been well decribed by Rensis Likert, who developed a "linking pin" theory to explain communications within the corporate hierarchy.[1] According to Likert, the hierarchical structure of a corporation can be broken down into a series of smaller hierarchies, with each superior within a subhierarchy managing several subordinates. The heads of each subhierarchy are in turn subordinates in another, larger hiearchy, hence the "linking pin" analogy.

The quality of communicaton within the hiearchy depends on the linking-pin communicator. This person is responsible for the flow of information up and down the hierarchy, and therefore communication across different levels is only as good as this individual allows it to be. If the linking-pin managers distort or block information, the organization may become uncoordinated in both its activity and its output.

Obviously, the impact of poor communicators anywhere in the hierarchy will have multiple repercussions. Information will not flow beyond them, and consequently, other members within their groups may be left in the dark about important facts that affect their work. But in the case of linking-pin managers, this becomes doubly important because of their role in coordinating the efforts of different groups.

Linking-pin managers, then, are key communicators. They must be relied upon to transmit information accurately and effectively, and they must control the amount of information that they allow to be transmitted. Their abilities in these respects are perhaps their primary qualifications for their positions of responsibility.

The issue of how much information is to be transmitted through the hierarchy should not be taken lightly. I have been associated with people whom I am sure have not been made managers because they talk too much. They tend to ramble on and do not edit what they say. In spite of their obvious brilliance, they cast an impression of being disorganized, and consequently they have been passed over on countless occasions when it came to promotion.

If you analyze your own reaction carefully, you will probably find that you tend to respect the professional manager who is able to control the stimuli in specific situations. And this is true not only in management, but in everyday life as well. Long before I entered the business field, I had an experience that illustrated this fact. At the time, I was a junior in college, and a fraternity brother who was being visited by his family invited me out to dinner. The restaurant to which we were taken was very expensive, and just thinking about the money these people were going to pay made me somewhat shy. Consequently, I did not speak very much, but my fraternity brother's sister spoke all night. In fact, I remember thinking to myself that she spoke so much that she didn't even eat her veal parmigiana.

The surprise happened the next day, when my fraternity brother came running up to me to tell me how impressed his sister was with me—and I had done nothing to impress her, except for noting that she wanted to talk and being too shy to interrupt.

As I reflect on some of the most charismatic managers to whom I have been exposed, it appears that their knowing how much or little to say is particularly important in assessing their qualities of leadership. Somehow, persuasive individuals say just the right amount of the right things. Their explanations may be crisp or long, soft or loud, angry or soothing, but in every case, they seem to have administered the required medicine to the business session.

In summary, there can be no doubt that proper control of communications is one of the critical responsibilities of modern-day managers. They must know how much to say in a given situation, and they must motivate the members of their group to pass on the adequate amount of information. A poor flow of information will result in understimulation and low levels of creativity and productivity; and an uncontrolled flow of communications will bring overstimulation, confusion, and inflexibility of the organization. To fulfill their function, managers must staff and organize their groups so that the ideal amount of stimulations can occur.

Managing Problem Solutions

Problems are solved by people, and to manage problem solutions means to manage people and their interactions. In a sense, this is but an extension of what we said in the previous section. When people interact to solve a problem, they build up stimuli. The more people involved, the more stimuli and the lower the likelihood of a simple problem solution under these conditions. It is doubly important to ensure that communications are properly controlled.

Of course, even with an inadequate flow of information through the hierarchy, it is possible either that the information required for a problem solution will be incorrect or that the wrong people will be working on the problem. These are additional factors that need to be controlled, although they will not be discussed in this section.

What is at stake here can be clarified by examining some of the classical theories about the flow of information within an organization.

We have already discussed Likert's "linking pin" theory, which emphasized the critical role of the manager in ensuring that communications flow from level to level within the hierarchy. This view is complemented by the conclusions reached in an earlier study by Henri Fayol.[2] Fayol proposed a "gangplank theory," which says that communications should travel horizontally at the lowest possible hierarchy level. Clearly, this would shorten the chain of command involved in transmitting specific messages, thereby increasing the efficiency of communication and decision making.

Most of us have probably experienced the joy and the ease of operations associated with such a special situation. It is a pleasure to be able to derive a problem solution without the picayune questioning of a supervisor or the delay brought about by a seemingly irresponsible signature approval list. However, more recent studies suggest that the gangplank theory in its original form is oversimplified and needs to be modified in certain ways.

To anticipate the results of these studies, it appears that (1) the extent and direction of communications within work groups must be controlled depending on the nature of the specific task at hand, and (2) under certain circumstances, the omission of senior people from the chain of communication will render the organization less efficient. The second conclusion follows from the obvious fact that when senior people lack knowledge about the activities of their subordinates, they become unable to lead the organization.

The work revealing these conclusions has been performed by Harold Leavitt[3] and by Harold Guetzkow and Herbert Simon.[4] These researchers examined the problem-solving capabilities of a group under conditions where the ability of its members to communicate with one another was limited.

Leavitt restricted communications so that they could take only certain directions. This is shown in Figure 3, in which people are symbolized as letters and communication channels as straight lines

Figure 3. The Leavitt system for analyzing the efficiency of communication patterns.

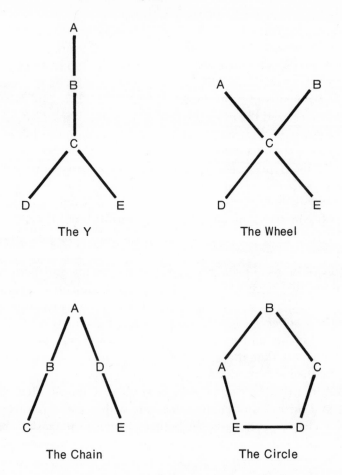

connecting them. Leavitt designed his experiments so that people could only communicate as in the patterns shown in the figure. For instance, in the Y group, people A and C could not communicate directly but only through B. Similarly, D and E in the same group could both communicate with C but not with each other.

In the simplest experiments of Leavitt, each member within a communication network group was given a card containing six symbols. One of the six symbols was the same for each of the people in the group. The task which they were assigned was to identify the common symbol. Competitive tests were performed, and data were collected on the time required for problem solution, the correctness of the solution, and the attitudes of the subjects.

The wheel group, in which all communications must go through a leader, showed the fewest errors and the fastest results. Unfortunately, when members of this group were asked how they liked their job, results showed that they were unhappy. The group found to enjoy the work most was the circle group, which had no leader. As can be seen from the figure, in the circle group, each member was allowed to talk with his two closest neighbors, and no one was assigned to a superior position.

Leavitt also gave each group a more difficult chore, namely to identify a common characteristic of multi-colored marbles that were handed out to the members. It was found that in this case, the circle group solved the problem faster.

The circle system, representative of participative management, is the formal management style usually recommended in cases where either problems are complex or people are highly educated and motivated. In this management style, people are free to communicate without the influence of a superior who might restrict the freedom of their thinking.

Leavitt's experiments indicate that work groups must be organized to fit the task at hand. If it is a simple task, then a management structure that relies on a leader will be most effective for completing the task. This is reminiscent of the factory conditions in the days of management by pressure. Conversely, to perform well on more complex problems, the use of a manager to control the flow of information seems neither required nor desirable.

We can conclude from this that one of the important tasks of the manager is to arrange the group according to the nature of the job to be performed. As in other areas of business life, there is a living, flexible aspect to problem resolution. Any group encounters simple as well as complex problems, and at all times there must be a judgment as to the nature of leadership required for a particular situation.

Leavitt's findings were confirmed by Guetzkow and Simon who added yet another group structure, called the all-channel system, in which no restrictions whatsoever were allowed between communicating individuals. The structures studies by these authors are depicted in Figure 4.

Figure 4. Guetzkow and Simon's models of restricted communication patterns.

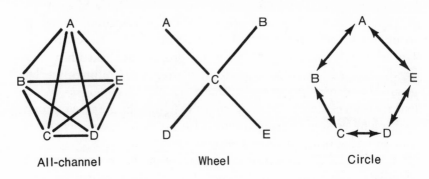

All-channel   Wheel   Circle

Guetzkow and Simon analyzed how the group's internal structure affects its performance on specific tasks. The central hypothesis explored by them was that unrestricted communications make it more difficult for a group to organize itself efficiently for task performance. In other words, according to their hypothesis, the chore of deciding with whom to work and communicate constitutes an additional work task that decreases the group's efficiency in solving a given problem. Without a leader, there are too many communication opportunities, and consequently there are too many stimuli.

The wheel group, as we have seen, represents a typical structure where there is a leader who exerts strong control over communications. At the other extreme, the all-channel group involves a situation with no leader and an unlimited number of stimuli. Guetskow and Simon's study confirmed that the wheel group solved problems faster. The authors concluded that although current management literature on the topic of communication leaves one with the expectation that a reduction of communication restrictions should lead to a better functioning organization, their findings indicate that unlimited freedom in communications is unwarranted.

The studies that we have just reviewed all point toward an important responsibility of managers interested in establishing a synergistic work environment: They must tailor communications within their groups to the specific problem to be solved. If the task is simple, they should exert control so as to maximize the efficiency of the group. On the other hand, if the group is faced with a complex problem, the restrictions on communications must be minimized so as to allow maximum cross-fertilization of ideas. Of course, even in such a relatively unstructured situation, the group leader may have to step in and demand disciplined attention if it becomes apparent that the group is not focusing on the issue in question.

In discussing the manager's task of controlling communications, it is important to realize that communication plays a critical role not only in influencing the thinking of other people but also in controlling the level of thinking and the number of induced stimuli in the communicator himself. The number of self-induced stimuli appears to vary from one individual to another, but we can assume that they are on a lower level of consciousness than stimuli introduced by overt verbal communications. Clearly, the mind focuses more sharply on ideas that have been verbally expressed than on thoughts that remain entirely internal. Communication, then, not only drives the number of stimuli to which people are exposed, it also helps sharpen ideas and problems by bringing them to a higher level of consciousness.

Properly controlled communications, we can conclude, facilitate problem solving in two important ways. One, they provide an adequate number of stimuli for the members of a work group. Two, they ensure that each group member is in the right state of mind—the most rational one. Indirectly, this also optimizes the chances of generating synergy because success in creative problem solving, as we have seen, is an important factor in bringing about resonance and the enjoyment of work that goes along with it.

If we were interested in organizing our environment so that harmonious (or "resonating," if you will) conversations can take place, we might worry a good deal less about the issue of controlling communications. More than this, there is no reason to believe that conversations will be more "successful" (however that is to be measured) if they are kept on a high level of consciousness. It is entirely possible that people derive more satisfaction from talking about whatever comes to their minds without having to pay attention to the purpose of their contributions. In fact, as I said in the introduction to this book, I found it very useful to institute "purposeless meetings," during which people can air their views and concerns freely without having to worry about the functional value of what they say.

However, in the typical corporate situation we are dealing not with simple conversations but with interactions aimed at creative solutions to often complex problems. Now creativity involves something more than communication; it implies a subtle balance of the number of stimuli with which the mind is involved at any given time. If there are too many, the mind will be driven so far into its subconscious that there will be no control of the direction of the thoughts. If there are too few, on the other hand, there may be insufficient input to achieve integration, which involves combining a number of stimuli or concepts into new patterns. We must make sure, therefore, that there will be neither overstimulation nor understimulation.

There are two aspects to our problem of control. One, we must determine, within reason, what the proper number of stimuli for each individual is. Two, because the number of stimuli depends to a great extent on the number of people in a group, we must address the question of the ideal size of work groups.

There is some experimental evidence that verifies the idea that there is an ideal number of stimuli for the efficient interaction of people within an organization. Donald Pelz and Frank Andrews studied the number of ideas generated in research laboratories as a function both of the educational degrees of the people in the laboratory and of the number of projects on which they worked.[5] We can interpret "educational degrees" and "number of projects" as being related directly to stimuli, because they determine the number of concepts with which the individuals had to cope.

In order to establish a quantitative base for their study, Pelz and Andrews judged the number of ideas (or, for our purposes, the degree of creativity exhibited) by seeking opinions about the creativity of the people involved from the group members themselves and also from their colleagues, subordinates, superiors, and higher executives. Their study provides a wealth of interesting data. In particular, it showed that creativity was highest when three Ph.D.'s were working in a laboratory in a situation where they were not dominated by other Ph.D's. Furthermore, it was found that Ph.D.'s were most creative when they were working on approximately four different projects simultaneously.

Although Pelz and Andrews' study was restricted to Ph.D.'s and specific conditions, we can probably generalize that maximum creativity can be achieved by mixing three people each of whom possesses specialized information, and by assigning each of them to four projects at a time. Of course, we must expect significant variations because of the differences in mental activity among individuals. In any case, it is clear that managers who are truly interested in creating synergy must limit the size of their work group and the number of projects given to each individual, or the chances for creativity will be poor at best.

Organizing for Synergy

As the discussion in the previous section suggests, a group leader should manage no more than three or four people. Interestingly enough, this hypothesis is supported by studies of group dynamics as well as by more abstract mathematical theories. In each case, the conclusion points to the need to avoid large groups.

William Scott deduced the ideal size of a group by examining the interactions among the people in a group.[6] He examined groups of two, three, four, five, and six people and noted the problems with each. In general, he concluded that with too few people, excessive tension develops, and with too many people, there is a tendency to divide into smaller groups. The right number of people is somewhere in between.

In looking at two-member groups, Scott noted that people who are forced to cooperate tend to produce tension because they are forced to form a working coalition and lack a third party against whom they can build up antagonism. In such a dyadic relation, the balance of power is very unstable because of potential unresolved tensions between the two members. Also, such groups do not provide for an "arbitrator" who could force the resolution of disruptive tensions. In short, then, the two-member group does not appear to be the basic building block of corporate hierarchies.

By contrast, groups of three people are much more stable. They have the extra person against whom emotions can be vented, and consequently, the relations in such groups are less sensitive. Also, disagreements can usually be resolved through a democratic vote, with a majority of two overrriding a single dissenter.

However, there is also a significant danger in having groups of this size. If the outvoted person is always the same, that person may withdraw from the triad relationship, and the relation may degenerate to a dyadic relationship with all its problems. For this reason, it is important to make sure that the same person will not be the adversary in every communication sequence. In practice, this may pose a real problem, and it indicates that there is more to synergistic management than merely selecting the right number of people. Group leaders must be aware of the personal characteristics and weaknesses of their subordinates, and they must know how to manage around them.

The problems discussed for three-member groups might lead one to expect that groups comprising four people are superior. However, Scott's analysis of groups of this size indicates that there can be a high degree of disagreement and antagonism among group members, culminating in a tendency toward deadlock between pairs of members. In that case, the group, if it is allowed to continue, is reduced to two dyadic relationships, both of which suffer from the kinds of deficiencies described earlier.

According to Scott, the five-member group shows much greater stability. This group is small enough to provide for easy interactions, yet there are enough people pooling resources to provide the necessary input for creative problem solving and efficient decision making. Furthermore, in disagreements, there is the overruling influence of a 3:2 split, and there is also a tendency for a leader to emerge. It may be concluded from Scott's arguments that a group of five is the minimum stable configuration. It overcomes all of the obstacles that were cited for groups of two, three, or four people.

Groups of six people will under stress reduce to three dyadic or two triadic relationships. But even if this barrier is overcome, stimuli will be difficult to control. Because of these two negative factors, groups of this size are less suitable than five-member groups. Similarly, the seven-member group tends to suffer from overstimulations, which will render the group inefficient.

In conclusion, then, Scott recommends that five people be involved in a work group—slightly more than we might have expected from Pelz and Andrews' study. The discrepancy might be explained, however, if we consider the difference between the individuals used in the two studies. In particular we may assume that the optimum size for a group consisting of Ph.D.'s is smaller than for groups of people with less training and education, since the number of self-induced stimuli should be unusually high in the case of Ph.D's. In other words, the results of the two studies seem compatible with our thesis that there is an ideal number of stimuli to which any group may be exposed.

Further confirmation of the ideal number of subordinates within a group comes from a purely mathematical study undertaken by Graicunas.[7] Looking at nonroutine work as it exists in most organizations, Graicunas concluded that the ideal number of subordinates in a group would be four. He reached this conclusion by considering the number of reaction channels that are possible in groups of different sizes. He theorized that a supervisor with two subordinates would have to have six relationships within his or her span of attention. These include the relationships of the supervisor with each of the subordinates, the relationship of subordinate A to subordinate B, the relationship of subordinate B to subordinate A, and the group relationships when the subordinates are together.

Extrapolating from this analysis, Graicunas developed an equation that showed that with four subordinates, the number of relationships rises to 44, and with five to 100. Thus, adding a fifth subordinate, he notes, would cause a 125 percent increase in complexity for a 20 percent increase in the amount of work done. He concludes that only in special situations is it worthwhile to add this extra person.

It seems, therefore, that the ideal group should have four to five people. The important thing to note for our discussion is that resonance is unlikely to be generated in groups significantly larger than this.

All well and good, but in real life things do not work like this. More often than not, circumstances demand that people manage more than four subordinates. For example, I have seven immediate subordinates. This means that for all practical purposes, my work group has eight members. This seems highly inappropriate for a believer in synergy like myself, yet there seems no way around it. In one case, there are two subordinates instead of one because I believe that one of them will shortly mature to the manager position. In another, there are three managers instead of one, each responsible for manufacturing operations at a different site.

Even if you have to live with such problems, you can make it a policy to invite only four or five people to any given meeting. Ideally, you would want to alternate the people whom you invited so as to avoid tension. In my own case, I have noticed that the four whom I invite most frequently to my meetings are not those who would be suggested by the organization chart but rather those who together develop a resonant spirit. In fact, I have created a task force composed of these special people so that no ill feelings arise among the other members of the group. I believe that a good, resonant group requires a special balance, and once the human recipe that works has been found, I am reluctant to change it. Admittedly, though, this was dictated by practical considerations, and if at all possible, it should be avoided.

The ideal group composition is difficult to achieve and requires significant judgment on the manager's part, because some people will generally tend to generate more stimuli than others. If this is the case, they should be mixed with people who can be expected to contribute correspondingly less.

In this respect, it should be noted that the people who are likely to produce the greatest number of stimuli are not necessarily those with the strongest expertise in one or more areas but the ones who in addition look for pragmatic solutions. Also, it should be remembered that not every area of expertise of a given individual will be put to use in every situation. Depending on the problem at hand, a person with considerable knowledge in several fields may turn out to be a low contributor. To find the proper mix of people, then, the manager must know not only the people in the group, their backgrounds, and how they think, but also how the task in question will affect their behavior as producers of stimuli.

Finally, the contributions made by different experts depend not only on the problem being discussed but also on personal preferences. For example, you may have a special individual in your group who has two specialties—say, marketing and production control—of which he wishes to use only one. Suppose you are interested in eliciting this person's ideas on a production control issue. If you know that this person is reluctant to use his or her expertise in this area, you must be prepared to ask direct questions, set ground rules, and filter out responses that lead away from your topic. Furthermore, if you know this person to be moody and likely to react with hostility, you may have to prepare the arena carefully before proceeding. In short, synergistic management requires great tact and sensitivity.

Difficult as the managerial task of organizing work groups appears to be, it is often simplified by people's instinctive desire to secure the pleasant emotions associated with synergy. Because of this, a large group, if left to its own devices, will tend to subdivide into workable subgroups.

For example, a large group of stockholders will appoint a nominating committee to propose a board of directors. Similarly, if a large work group is faced with an analytical or planning problem, it will tend to assign a special task force to it. Instinctively, we recognize that when the number of people is too large, nothing tends to be accomplished, and so we divide into smaller groups. However, our instinctive understanding of the reasons for subdividing is not acute enough to bring about the ideal organization for arbitration, stimulation, and ease of communication. That vague intuition must be supplemented by alert management.

As we have seen in our review of Pelz and Andrews' study, there is need to control not only the size of work groups but also the number of projects assigned to each individual. The amount of stimuli to which the group is exposed depends on both factors. Now, the natural tendency for managers is to load their people with work so that they are well saturated with responsibilities. For instance, if MBO is being employed, every goal on the organization's "shopping list" tends to be listed. But if people are to work on these objectives systematically rather than achieve them by chance, then it is imperative that the number of objectives be limited.

From the preceding discussion, we can conclude that to maximize the chances of creative contributions, employees should work on four or five objectives at a time. This number, incidentally, is compatible with the four or five technical specialties that are required—as implied by Pelz and Andrews' study—if an individual is to be creative in technical pursuits. And it agrees with the optimum number of people who can work together to generate ideas in a brainstorming session. In conclusion, although there is limited hardcore evidence supporting the thesis that four or five objectives is the ideal number with which an individual should be concerned, there is good reason to believe that this is the case.

Limiting objectives is in itself a task that requires creative problem solving and conflict resolution. Typically, each person will bring more than four objectives to an objective-setting session, some of which have to be eliminated.

In the simplest form, we might opt for a compromise solution: I'll give up some of my objectives if you do the same. This may be appropriate for objectives of limited importance. Generally, however, an integrative solution is to be preferred. This calls for creative combining of different objectives so that a workable number of tasks can be established.

Let me give an example. A subordinate once sought my approval for a list of ten or so objectives. He was a research manager, and among his objectives were (1) to develop two new products, each with sales potentials in excess of $200,000 by year end, and (2) to develop an innovative manufacturing technique that would increase our production capacity twofold without requiring significant capital expenditures.

At the time, his second objective appeared essential since we were operating at full capacity on our major facilities. Pressed by the need to reduce the overall number of objectives to a manageable minimum, we discovered that the two objectives mentioned above could be combined in a meaningful way to read: "Develop two new products, each with sales potentials of over $200,000, and each utilizing low-demand manufacturing facilities."

In this case, the exercise of combining objectives forced us to solve the problem of increasing production capacity while arriving at a better definition of the new products that had to be developed. In other words, this simple exercise enabled us to give better direction to our research and development effort and at the same time to simplify our tasks.

Reducing the number of objectives to be achieved not only is essential to synergistic management, it also is a necessity of good planning. More often than not, blind adoption of a multitude of objectives means that there will be unnecessary duplication of efforts. By combining related objectives and coordinating activities correspondingly, the group will be working more effectively.

We have seen, then, that managers interested in synergy must expend considerable energy on establishing and maintaining a work group that is conducive to resonance and creative problem solving.

First, they must hire people whom they can trust and who not only exhibit a high degree of creativity but also show a quality of moderation—a sense of proportion, if you will. They must know how to develop and maintain trust, and this starts at home: They must be trustworthy themselves and be willing to get to know their people's capabilities, attitudes, and personal characteristics. This cannot be done without a continuous dialog.

Secondly, they must make sure that communications proceed through the hierarchy as needed. On one hand, this involves trust that people will transmit messages without undue distortions and will be thoughtful enough to restrict the amount of information they pass on to a minimum. On the other hand, it requires active control of the size and composition of the group and of the number of projects assigned to each member.

These are not problems that permit a mechanical approach. To maintain a reasonable level of stimulation in the group, the manager must take into account the task at hand as well as the personal characteristics of the people involved. High contributors of stimuli should be offset by low contributors, and the structure of the group should allow for arbitration and cross-fertilization of ideas. Where the situation demands groups comprising more than the ideal five members, compatible subgroups should be organized for specific tasks.

Finally, the number of objectives to be worked on should be reduced to four or five for each individual, not by a simple process of elimination, but by a creative integration of related tasks.

NOTES

1. Likert, Rensis, *The Human Organization*, New York: McGraw-Hill, 1967.
2. Fayol, Henri, *General and Industrial Management*, Translated from the French by Constance Sturrs, London: Sir Isaac Pitman & Sons, Ltd., 1949.
3. Leavitt, Harold J., "Some Effects of Certain Communication Patterns on Group Performance," *Journal of Abnormal and Social Psychology*, 1951.
4. Guetzkow, Harold, and Herbert A. Simon, "The Impact of Certain Communication Nets Upon Organization and Performance in Task Oriented Groups," *Management Science* 1, 1955.
5. Pelz, Donald C., and Frank M. Andrews, *Scientists in Organizations*, New York: John Wiley and Sons, 1966.

6. Scott, William G., *Organization Theory*, Homewood, Ill.: Richard D. Irwin, 1967.
7. Graicunas, V. A., "Relationships in Organizations," *Papers on the Science of Administration*, L. Gulick and L. Urwick (eds.), New York: Institute of Public Administration. Also in *Management*, Paul E. Torgerson and Irwin T. Weinstock (eds.), Englewood Cliffs, N.J.: Prentice-Hall, 1972.

People Barriers

6

Having said this much, it would seem that to reap the rewards of synergy, all that is left to do is to apply the principles set forth in the preceding chapters. Unfortunately, things are not that simple.

There has been a tacit assumption in our theory that needs elaboration, namely that people, if given a chance to do so, will relate to each other in a way that creates resonance. But even a brief look at interactions among people makes it clear that this is usually not the case. Communications between people tend to break down, because of various barriers, before resonance can be achieved. Synergistic management must take these barriers into account and counteract them.

Perhaps the emotion of resonance is not experienced by most of us because we do not have the sensitivity to *anticipate* it. This anticipation of an imminent emotion is particularly difficult to achieve, and it is just as difficult to explain. Analogous phenomena are familiar from the physical sciences. For example, significant scientific speculation has been expended in analyzing how lightning "knows" the route of minimum resistance *before* it has struck—how it discovers the hidden conductors that give it a secure route to the ground. Explaining such anticipatory phenomena seems to be significantly easier than explaining the anticipatory performance of people who are blessed—or cursed—with the most complex mental system that we know of.

Nonetheless, it seems important to take a closer look at this problem because it bears directly on the success or failure of synergistic management. Although a full study of this issue is beyond the scope of this book, some initial insights into the way an emotion is anticipated can be gained by extending the theory of Transactional Analysis (TA).

TA has been promoted as a suitable way to analyze the communications between people, and many of its features shed light on the question of why and under what circumstances communication breaks down.

Fundamentals of Transactional Analysis

In my opinion, the most important contributions to TA have been made by Eric Berne[1] and Thomas Harris.[2] Whereas Harris's work is concerned with the basics of TA, Berne specifically addressed the question of how this theory can be used to analyze the communication interplay between people. This is particularly valuable to us because before we can show how TA helps explain some of the common barriers to resonance, we must have a broad understanding of what goes on when people communicate.

In TA, each personality is analyzed as a combination of three different roles. People oscillate between these different personality types, depending on the combined stimuli to which they are exposed at any one time. These three ego states are the Parent, the Adult, and the Child. The interaction between people is explained in terms of whether they respond as Adults, Children, or Parents.

The Child personality has its roots in the preadolescent period, probably prior to the age of five, when the parent exerted the greatest pressure on the development of the child. TA proponents theorize that the emotional responses learned during this period persist in the mind of the adult and commonly surface as one particular way of reacting to stimuli.

The characteristic feature of the Child personality is the predominance of *emotions*, which lack logic and moderation. Furthermore, there is a general feeling of inferiority within this personality, which is a result of all the demands that have been made on the child as he grew up. In particular, this negative orientation stems from the strong discipline to which the child was subjected, for example, the toilet training, the forced feeding, or forced napping.

These negative factors are only partially offset by the positive aspects of this personality—creativity, curiosity, and the desire to explore, touch, feel, and generally gather experience.

The symptoms of the Child personality include tears, quivering, pouting, temper tantrums, downcast eyes, shrugging shoulders, teasing, delight, and laughter. Child words include "I wish," "I want," "I don't know," "I don't care."

The Child state seems to correspond to the id of Freudian psychology. According to classical explanations, the id includes two opposite drives—love and hate—and is governed by repressed memories and experiences and primitive wishes and impulses.

In one organization for which I worked, there was a secretary who appeared to be the perfect example of a personality that continuously operated as a Child. You could hear her giggle permeate the hallway, shudder at her continuous dialog regarding "cute" people, and despair about her continuous concern over play and fun and her emotional outbreaks if things didn't go her way. You will probably have little trouble identifying more subtle examples of this personality style that must exist in your own organization.

Like the Child state, the characteristic personality of the Parent personality is developed during the first five years of life. It includes those responses that the child observed in his parents, in particular, disciplinary behavior, and it appears to be influenced by the way the child felt about the discipline to which he was exposed.

The parent was an authority figure, and consequently, the Parent state is one of superiority, authority, and command. Because this personality was acquired at a time when the child was unable to evaluate the parents' behavior in a critical, objective way, the Parent-type responses that are carried over into adulthood do not allow for editing or questioning of any kind. In other words, they are simply *copied* behavior patterns that are committed to memory in uninterpreted form.

Common behavior in the Parent ego state is the citing of illogical rules that may have been learned during early childhood, when the parent was overly concerned about the safety of the child. Consequently, you may diagnose as Parent behavior excessive use of *no*'s, *don'ts*, or other illogical absolutes. Also the illogical possessive love that the parent shows toward the child can be interpreted as a signal of this ego state.

Clues to the Parent personality include furrowed brow, pursed lips, foot tapping, hands on hips, arms folded across the chest, wringing hands, and even patting others on the head. Verbally, the Parent reacts with strong disciplinarian statements like "I am going to put a stop to this," "How many times have I told you?" "If I were you," and so on.

The Parent ego state corresponds most closely with the superego of Freudian psychology. The superego is said to incorporate four components: (1) the rules that have been taught to the child; (2) the values that have been handed down, including religious and moral concepts; (3) the ego ideal—the preconceived, illogical notion of what the ego should be; (4) the internal judging-policing function—the Jimminy Cricket of Pinocchio, or, less colloquially, the conscience. When rules are broken, the Parent personality generates feelings of guilt, regardless of whether or not they are logical.

As with the Child ego state, you probably know people whose personality is dominated by Parent-like characteristics. More often than not, they are easily manipulated by anybody who is able to adjust his own behavior to their personality. I have been associated with one individual who strikes me as such a case. He would sit in meetings, with his arms crossed, his chin on his chest, waiting for an opportunity to act "father." To get this gentleman's approval, which was a *sine qua non*, you had to appeal to his Parent personality. Provided you were willing to talk up to him and ask for help or play hurt, his approval was almost automatic, and the grapevine was quick to invent effective rules for working with this man.

The Parent and Child personalities are in contrast with the Adult ego state. The Adult is the mature, objective personality that allows individuals to act on the basis of their own awareness and original thoughts. It develops as the child learns the difference between thought and feelings. Adult responses are based on information that is internally absorbed and analyzed.

The Adult may be likened to a computer, which formulates

logical decisions after processing the appropriate data. There are three functions of the Adult personality that we can isolate. First, it edits the emotional responses of the person, making sure that they are appropriate to the situation. Secondly, it weighs alternatives, assigns probabilities of success and failure to particular decisions, and steers the self in its actions. Finally, it is the source of creativity. Creativity is born in the curiosity of the Child personality, but the Child provides only the basic drive; the Adult provides the how.

The Adult personality is associated with continuous movement of the face, the eyes, and the body. Basic Adult words include curiosity satisfiers like why, what, where, when, who, and how; and Adult phrases include fact-oriented expressions like "as we stated before" or "it has been observed."

The Adult of TA seems to correspond with Freud's ego. According to Freudian psychology, the ego controls drives and directs the pressures of the id. It is characterized by its ability to concentrate, judge, and formulate creative solutions.

Analyzing Transactions

People's communications can be analyzed in terms of which personality—the Adult, the Parent, or the Child—addresses which ego state in the respondent. According to TA, if a transaction is "complementary," discourse is likely to continue without psychological barriers. Complementary transactions are those in which both participants agree on the relationship governing the communication. For instance, if A assumes the role of the Parent and B responds as a Child, the transaction is complementary (Figure 5a). On the other hand, if B responded as an Adult or a Parent, lines would cross, and the communication would be likely to break down (Figure 5b).

Even with complementary transactions, communication will eventually break down unless there is an Adult-Adult relationship. For instance, a Parent-Child transaction in which the Parent asserts, "It is against corporate policy" and the Child insists, "I want it" can last only as long as the partners can persist in repeating the same message again and again. Possibly, the Parent might vary his response by stating, "You will get in trouble," or

Figure 5. Complementary *(a)* **and crossed** *(b)* **transactions.**

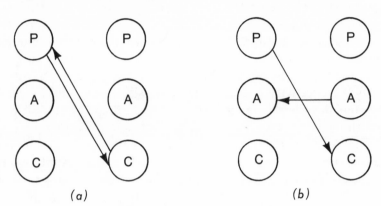

(a)   (b)

the Child might respond with the variant "Let's do it just once," but essentially, these are learned, stereotyped responses that cannot lead to a fruitful extended dialog.

The situation is somewhat improved if one of the partners assumes the Adult role. Being creative, the Adult can add new stimuli to the verbal intercourse even if the other partner begins to run out of learned Child or Parent responses. However, even such transactions will eventually lead to breakdown because the creative output of the Adult alone will usually be inadequate for an enduring exchange. To put it in our terms, because of the inflexibility of the Child to adapt responses to the particular communication situation, resonance will not occur, and the communication will remain unsuccessful.

In order to enjoy the benefits of resonance, then, it is necessary to have Adult-Adult communications, in which both partners remain flexible in their responses and retain a mature, objective attitude. In such exchanges, the "communicative lines" do not cross, which avoids deadlocks because of a perceived role conflict, and each person's responses remain adjusted to the needs of the situation.

Unfortunately, people cannot be relied on to behave continuously as Adults. In the normal course of events, they will fluctuate between different roles, and this must be anticipated and patience must be exercised if resonance is to result. Nonetheless, both partners should strive to keep the interchange at a predominantly Adult level.

Let me illustrate our point about role switching with an example. Suppose you offended a colleague by saying something that was construed in the wrong way. Your colleague responds by ignoring you, and consequently you explain to him what you meant by your misconstrued statement, apologize for it, and ask how you can make amends. Surely this is an Adult response. Suppose now that the other person says something like, "You always talk without considering others." He basically talks to you as a parent would, and he wants you to behave like a child, put your head down, and maybe even pout. But you do not want to do that. You have apologized in a mature way, and to go beyond that, you feel, is unnecessary.

Perhaps you try again to settle the situation by restructuring your apology. Your apology is not accepted. The other man talks like a parent to a child, scolding you for what you did. By this time, you might get mad and tell your colleague that he is acting in an immature way. If that happens, you have switched to the Parent role. Each parent is talking to a child; there is no listening, and the communication will terminate in short order. This type of exchange is shown in Figure 5a earlier in this section. According to TA, when the transaction lines cross as in Figures 5a and 5b, communications usually break down.

This same situation might have led to a "resonant" exchange if instead of yourself switching to the Parent role, you could have persuaded the other person to adopt an Adult behavior. In that case, instead of chiding you like a parent, he might have seen your perspective, stated that he understood what had happened, and perhaps asked you why it had happened. If both of you could have persisted in the Adult-Adult mode, it would have been only a matter of time before resonance would result.

Adult-Adult transactions represent communications involving the creative capacities of people, and if the relationship remains on this level, then creative ideas will ordinarily result, increasing the chances of resonance.

Of course, it is possible to talk for a time in this mode and have nothing happen. For example, you may ask about the level of sales for the last month, hear that it was $1,000,000, and say "thank you." Obviously, this is somewhat short of resonance—something still appears to be missing. Possibly both parties are too preoccupied with other problems to invest in this particular exchange. Or the subject matter of their conversation is of limited interest and therefore does not provide any motivation to seize the opportunity and work on establishing resonance.

Even in such cases, however, the transaction may have contributed to the development of resonance. We can expect that each Adult-Adult exchange will improve the nature of communications between the parties, leaving a residual effect that increases the chances of synergy. Therefore, the energy put into keeping transactions at an Adult-Adult level is well invested even when the occasion seems trivial at the moment.

In this connection, it is worth mentioning that the extent to which a particular interaction contributes to establishing resonance is not necessarily determined by the amount of time expended on it. I remember being associated with a man who was a director of the Rochester Sales Executive Club at the same time as myself. We used to talk about various things as need dictated. On one memorable occasion we were taking a course together in Jungian Analysis, and we had to interview each other. Five minutes were allowed for this exercise, and it was striking how much better we knew each other after this short session than after all the conversations we had had before. The point is that casual conversations often seem extremely inefficient in bringing about emotional ties. It is the depth rather than the duration of a communication that decides the value of a transaction for generating synergy.

Introverts and Extroverts

We have seen, then, that to achieve resonance, it is important to keep transactions at the Adult-Adult level, which affords the greatest opportunities for mature and creative responses. Transactional Analysis seems an adequate tool for explaining the mental attitudes of people as they interact. However, it is not necessarily true that there is a direct correlation between what people think and what they do. Two people having an Adult-Adult conversation may well have the right ideas and even sense the possibility of resonance, yet fail to make it a reality.

For instance, one of the partners may have an idea that would contribute critically to a creative problem solution, but at the same time this person may lack the self-confidence to communicate it. This is true especially for the early stages of a transaction, when inhibitions have not yet been torn down. As the anticipatory feeling of resonance grows stronger, we may find the same bashful person contributing his or her ideas with a megaphone.

The point of this is that we all edit to some extent the things we say or do. We do not do all the things we think of doing, and we do not say everything that comes to our minds. Of course, this editing function is less prominent in some people than in others. At the one extreme, we have the extrovert, who seems incapable of suppressing any thought or feeling; at the other, we have the introvert, who edits everything to excess.

It seems safe to say that over 50 percent of the American people are introverts. The introvert tends to say little, be reluctant to shout, sit in a stiff posture, laugh softly, look away when shaking hands, have difficulty in making cocktail party conversation, and generally assume passive roles. To be regarded as an introvert, you do not have to exhibit all these characteristics. In fact, introverted behavior is best measured along a continuous scale from normal to extreme.

The behavioral characteristics of the extrovert are just the opposite of those of introverts. Extroverts tend to be loud, talk continuously, and assume active roles. In short, they are less self-conscious than introverts.

It would probably be a mistake to assume that the introvert and the extrovert *think* differently. Beneath their overt behavior, their mental processes may in fact be very similar. What does seem to be different is their reaction to their thoughts, which determines to what exten*t* they communicate them. The fact remains, however, that both introverts and extroverts can create serious barriers to communication and to resonance.

The bad habit that seems to be at the root of the introvert's personality is the inability or unwillingness to verbalize the concepts that are generated by his mind. Saying what is on your mind is in large part a habit, and the introvert has simply failed to develop it. It seems reasonable to assume that the introvert's attitude was developed in early childhood. As we are all aware, many parents tend to encourage their children toward this kind of behavior. For example, children are encouraged to be quiet and taught not to interrupt adults when they are speaking, and even the volume level of their laughter and the duration of their crying may be subject to control. By the same token, the child may be criticized for illogical statements or disorganized jumping from topic to topic. This fear of criticism appears to be carried over into adulthood, where it leads to excessive editing of thoughts.

Extroverts, it would seem, have been exposed to such parental discipline to a lesser degree. Being less self-conscious and not having been taught to think rather than speak, they tend to be extreme verbalizers. And this is exactly why they too tend to create barriers to resonance. Whatever is on the extrovert's mind is expressed. If his thoughts repeat, he will be repetitive in his speech; if his thoughts jump from subject to subject, he will tend to jump from subject to subject in his statements. In short, the extrovert needs to learn some of the "bad" habits of the introvert: He must learn to say less or edit the things about which he talks.

There are two obvious ways in which extroverts create a barrier to resonance. One, they tend to disrupt the thinking of other people. Two, and just as important, they shut off stimuli to themselves, thereby depriving themselves of the input they require to develop their full creativity.

Our best thinking is done under closely controlled conditions. For some people, this might mean a Mozart recording blaring away, a room of screaming kids, or the rhythm of a typewriter clicking. Few of us, however, can work with the constant talk of an extrovert demanding our attention. Creative thinking requires a delicate balance of stimuli from the conscious and from the subconscious, and to respond to an extrovert's continuous chatter, apart from demanding most of our time, forces us into an exclusively conscious mode.

People commonly protect themselves against this invasion into the private world of their thoughts by totally ignoring the extrovert. The mind is quite good at this sort of thing. While absorbed in thought, I have driven past my exit on the way to work, gone to a factory where I used to work, put shaving cream on my tooth brush, and ignored my boss in the supermarket. Although this is not easy to control, our mind can create seclusion to the point where we are almost totally dominated by internal signals.

As can be imagined, this situation, though common, is not conducive to an effective work environment. Instead, the manager must take steps to minimize the barriers created by extreme extroverts on the staff. This may involve controlling such people's contributions by establishing appropriate ground rules for meetings or, if that does not solve the problem, privately pointing out the need to consider other people's rights and needs. Clearly, this requires great tact and diplomacy, and the approach taken will to some extent depend on the personal characteristics of the people involved. The important point is that the manager must be sensitive to the problem and watch out for signs of disruptive extrovert behavior.

The mechanism by which the introvert prevents resonance is quite different. Introverts, in their private seclusion, do not provide their fair share of stimuli. By keeping their thoughts to themselves, they deprive the other members of the group of the benefits to which they are entitled.

From the manager's perspective, therefore, the problem with introverts is that they must be more strongly motivated before they will contribute their ideas to the group. This may seem like an impossible problem to solve, but actually, it becomes simpler once you understand the psychological factors that cause the introvert's behavior. The most important of these is probably fear, for as we have seen, introverts usually act the way they do because of a deep-seated desire, acquired in early childhood, to avoid criticism. Fear is a powerful motivator, and as a manager interested in synergy, you must detect its signs and take decisive steps to break down this barrier.

Fear as a Barrier to Resonance

If our hypothesis is correct, then introverts are shy for fear of being rejected; they feel inadequate because they anticipate criticism for not performing well; they take passive roles because they fear being rebuffed for being more aggressive; and they talk softly because they are afraid to disturb other people. In short, fear provides the simplest explanation to the many questions about introvert behavior.

A particularly interesting explanation of the mechanism by which fear influences the role that a person assumes is provided by Harry Levinson.[3] He identifies two important factors in the personality of every individual, the self-image and the "ego ideal."

According to my interpretation of his explanation, the ego ideal is a personal image that people have of themselves at their future best. It is formed from both the expectations that parents and others hold for a child and from the aspirations that the child develops for himself out of his recognition of his capabilities and his identification with important people in his environment. The ego ideal, then, is a distant goal toward which the psyche is continuously striving.

The self-image, on the other hand, is not nearly so lofty. It simply is a view of the self as it sees itself at the present time. It may include the realization that you are an above-average manager who is earning a fair wage but is not doing as well as the dumb kid in your class who graduated in the lowest 20 percent, yet lives for two months a year on his own $650,000 estate in Greece—without help from his father.

Levinson postulates that people's behavior is motivated mostly by the difference between their self-image and their ego ideal. The more the two differ and the stronger the ego ideal, the more likely it is that the individual will be highly motivated. His energies are directed at improving his self-image so as to minimize the gap between self-image and ego ideal.

Insofar as people do not take themselves lightly—and from my experience it seems that they do not—we must assume that their desire to achieve their ego ideal is associated with a deep-seated, often unconscious fear that they might fail in this quest. Consequently, they will tend to shy away from actions that they feel might increase the gap between what they believe they are and what they think they want to be. For example, a man on your staff may be reluctant to accept new responsibilities because he fears that he may be unable to live up to them and thereby ruin his chances of a promotion that he considers important.

As a manager, you must be sensitive to this problem. First of all, you must develop an idea of what your people are all about— how they view themselves and what their personal goals are. There may well be cases where a person's fears are justified, and you will be doing him a bad service by pushing him into directions that will lead him away from his goals. On the other hand, where fears are irrational, you should make an effort to get at their causes and make it clear that the course you propose holds no danger and is in the person's own best interest. For example, if you know that the person who resisted accepting increased responsibilities has all the capabilities to meet them, you may have to increase his confidence in his own potentials by pointing out his past successes and other qualifications.

Of course, our discussion of fear assumes that the more basic needs of an individual have been fulfilled. Abraham Maslow listed these basic needs by priority; they include things like food, a roof over the head, and association with other human beings.[4] There is no sense in considering the role of fear as a motivator when a person is starving, because under these conditions, his sole concern would be to find food to lessen his pain.

In the typical business situation, such basic needs are usually met, and we therefore need not be overly concerned with them here. It is unlikely that your subordinates are starving or live in total isolation or without a roof over their heads. Nonetheless, in milder form, you may have to pay some attention to such basic issues. For instance, you may find that a person's mind is absorbed by financial worries—mortgages, college expenses, alimony payments, or other obligations—or by concerns about inadequate housing or a thoroughly dissatisfying social life. If you are unaware of such problems, you may find yourself trying to motivate a particular subordinate with techniques that are simply aimed at the wrong level.

It all leads back to a point that has been made repeatedly: To make progress toward your goal of synergy, you must invest energies into finding out not only about people's abilities but also their psychology, their goals, and their personal problems.

Fear, then—excepting cases where people are concerned about fulfilling their basic material needs—is a barrier that is created entirely within the minds of people, for it relates to a perceived discrepancy between mental images that people have of themselves. Evidently, the introvert is cursed with more fears than the extrovert, but again, this appears to be an internal problem; it would make no sense to assume that the introvert is exposed to a greater share of real dangers than the extrovert. In addition, the reasons for fear often remain unsubstantiated. Chances are that you will not be fired if you speak up and that you will not disturb people more by walking into a room boldly than by tiptoeing in like an awkward ballerina. However, there are other situations where fear is the product of logical thought, and under these conditions it must be dealt with in a concrete way.

In the business environment there is relatively little danger of physical harm. For instance, it is unlikely that you will be physically assaulted because you spoke your mind. Rather, people's fears are related to the possibility of material damage. For example, the politics that are rampant in many organizations are a rational source of fear. They might result in the loss of a person's position, opportunities, money, or status.

This is a real problem that does not lend itself to quick and easy solutions. The political climate in an organization tends to be a deeply entrenched tradition, built up over the years, and its effects can be counteracted only by patient work. In fact, the great temptation is to assume a passive attitude and live with the situation.

Yet, it is up to the members of the organization to change things for the better, and there is no reason why you should not make a start. In essence, there are two routes that you can take, and both are realistically confined to your sphere of influence.

One, you can make an effort to stop political pressures from higher levels or other groups from penetrating your own group. This may require a certain ability to take a hard-nosed stand, but to my mind, this is one of the important qualities that distinguishes good managers from average ones.

Two—and this brings us back to one of the main topics of this book—you must establish an atmosphere of trust within your group. Your subordinates must be sure that they will not be subject to underhanded actions on your part, and they must be equally able to rely on the trustworthiness of their colleagues. In this last respect, remember that the manager of a group sets the tone: If he or she behaves in a trustworthy way and makes it clear that the same is expected of others, the group will move toward an atmosphere of openness and trust rather than of shady corporate politics.

The Trust Barrier

As we have seen in the previous chapter, trust plays an important role in managing communications. We have said there that you must be able to rely on your associates to transmit your messages without undue distortions and to exercise sound judgment as to what information to pass on and what to keep to themselves. If you cannot be sure of that, communications will grow out of control, and the creativity and productivity of your group will suffer.

It might be assumed that in our present discussion, we are dealing with trust in a somewhat different, perhaps more basic sense, because we were evidently concerned with the crippling impact of a lack of trust in people's decency and honesty on the transactions between different individuals. Yet, our discussion closely relates to the issue of communication, for the transactions we are interested in are communications between people. Accordingly, our point about lack of trust as a barrier to resonance can be summarized by saying that without trust, the stimuli generated by a group and communicated among its members will be inadequate and often distorted.

Some examples may help make our point clearer. Suppose that you are a salesman who has been laboring for many months over developing a new customer that shows potentials of placing an unusually large order. Suppose further that you have an associate whom you distrust. Perhaps you have seen this man operate, and you know that he has taken the commission from one of your associates. Your lack of trust, then, is not based on a figment of your imagination but is justified.

Under these circumstances, you will naturally be reluctant to tell your associate about the good fortune you had in your scouting activity of the day. But in doing this, you may be depriving yourself of stimuli from him that might have proved helpful. For instance, he might have come up with a sales argument that would have clinched the deal. He may even have personal contacts that would have been particularly helpful in this situation. In short, because there was a lack of trust, however justified, both you and the company may have lost an important opportunity that could have been seized if communications between you and your colleague had been intact.

To take another example, consider a case where you need the cooperation of associates without having the authority to order them to comply with your request. This is not an uncommon situation. I remember an occasion where in order to consolidate a sale, we needed to join forces with another plant within our company. By combining our resources, we would have been able to offer a package that could have been duplicated by no other company in the nation. Unfortunately, because of the structure of the company, the profit made on the job would have been assigned to my division, whereas the other group would have been paid for labor and overhead on a cost-plus basis.

A million-dollar venture was at stake, and still it was impossible to induce the other group to cooperate. The spirit that seemed to prevail was "You can only get in trouble if you stick your neck out"—evidently, trust was very much missing. From all I could surmise, the people whose cooperation I was trying to get must have been hurt in the past. Perhaps they had agreed to undertake a project that had originally been judged simple and inexpensive but turned out to involve considerable work and expenses at little return to the division. Whatever the facts, this group of people had obviously learned that they could save themselves anxiety by not committing themselves to certain tasks.

Obviously, when trust is missing to the extent that justifiable risks are not assumed, everybody loses out. The organization will miss important opportunities, and the individuals concerned will build up animosity toward each other. In short, lack of trust, which may begin as no more than a general *passive* attitude that stops people from getting involved, can start a powerful vicious circle of *active* dislikes and political intrigues.

I have experienced the effects of the trust barrier even among my own subordinates. One case, for instance, involved a salesman who seemed to lack the persistence and aggressiveness that are the mark of a good sales professional. Finally, when criticized for his negative attitude, he admitted that he acted the way he did because he feared being reprimanded for his aggressiveness. It turned out that his lack of trust was caused by a previous superior who had blocked his career because of his aggressive behavior. As a result of that experience, he obviously had gone to the other extreme.

If you find that trust is missing, you must keep in mind that you are dealing with a psychological problem that may not be solved by logical argument alone. For instance, in our last example it would probably not be enough merely to explain to the subordinate why his worries are unfounded; in general, such cases require patient, repeated efforts to build up the person's confidence and eliminate irrational fears. In the case of the salesman on my staff, for instance, I made a point of formally reviewing his progress each month.

I have tried several indirect techniques for overcoming the trust barrier, some of which might prove useful to others. In one case, I established a visitation schedule because I felt that frequent exposure would help build the social trust which is a preamble to work trust. In another case, I started an active campaign to "good-mouth" people who lacked trust. For instance, letters were sent to them acknowledging their efforts, and in cases where people performed exceptional work, special steps were taken to bring this to the attention of their superiors. On other occasions, people who had done good work for us were invited to join us on business trips so as to create opportunities for social interaction, as well as to expose them more directly to the needs and problems of our customers.

None of these techniques individually served as a cure-all for the general distrust that existed, but I like to believe that their combined effect contributed to the observed improvement in our relations with these people.

A word of caution: Establishing an atmosphere of trust, worthwhile as this goal is, should not become a sport. Your efforts should remain in proportion with the situation and with your chances of success. In cases where the harm done seems clearly irreversible or where people seem genuinely incompatible, it may sometimes be best to sever relationships with an employee so that he or she can find a more suitable environment.

Overcoming People Barriers

In this chapter, we have examined some of the common barriers to resonance that are created by people. As we have seen, people assume certain roles—the Parent, the Adult, or the Child—and although we all probably fluctuate between these three roles, most of us tend to be dominated in our behavior by a particular personality style.

To maximize the chances of creativity, managers should actively encourage the members of their group to keep transactions on an Adult-Adult level. Adult responses are mature, objective, and mediated by rational judgment; this distinguishes them from

Parent and Child responses, which are inflexible and stereotyped and therefore unlikely to lead to creative ideas.

Furthermore, the manager must watch out for signs of extreme introverted or extroverted behavior, for both can create additional barriers to resonance. Whereas extreme extroverts may have to be controlled to some extent so as to prevent disruptive overstimulation, introverts may have to be encouraged to overcome unjustified fears, or else they will fail to contribute their fair share of stimuli to the group.

The basic remedy for irrational fears, which we have recognized as a powerful motivator of people's behavior, is to establish an atmosphere of trust. This, as we will see, involves communicative skills. The way you talk, listen, write, and even gesture influences the image of yourself that you create in other people's minds. Similarly, your abilities to listen and read determine how accurate the images are that you form of others. These questions will occupy us in the next chapters.

NOTES

1. Berne, Eric, *What Do You Say After You Say Hello?*, New York: Grove Press, 1972.
2. Harris, Thomas A., *I'm OK, You're OK*, New York: Harper & Row, 1970.
3. Levinson, Harry, Public address, Rochester, N.Y., May 1974.
4. Maslow, Abraham H., *Motivation and Personality*, New York: Harper & Row, 1954.

Verbal Skills

7

Although there is an increased awareness of the importance of communicative skills in the business environment, the full impact of communication on the organization is often not recognized. Besides, there is a great gap between theory and practice: Many people who could give you an illuminating lecture on how to communicate with others will do a pitiful job at applying their theoretical knowledge.

In our context, we are interested in verbal skills as a prerequisite to achieving resonance and ultimately synergy. Ordinarily, this is not a direct process; resonance, as the discussion in the previous chapters indicates, presupposes trust, a common code, and rapid feedback, and these in turn depend on effective communications.

In this chapter, therefore, we will examine certain fallacies regarding verbal skills and indicate ways in which the manager can become a more effective communicator.

There are four false assumptions on which I would like to focus. Although they clearly do not exhaust the field, they appear the ones most commonly made by managers who may be quite proficient in many other respects. The false assumptions are (1) "If I write it, they will read it," (2) "If I say it, they will hear it," (3) "If I put it in writing, there will be no ambiguity," and (4) "Our communicative habits cannot be changed."

Any of these mistaken beliefs can endanger the success of a well-meant effort. In the following, we will discuss each of them in turn.

"If I Write It, They Will Read It"

In the corporate environment, there seem to be two major reasons why people do not read what has been written. In the first place, people are taught to skim as quickly as possible; in the second place, they are not motivated to read. The combination of these two factors may cause the addressee to miss important parts of the message over which you have toiled.

If every letter of every word were read, the average reading rate of a person, according to Paul Kolers, would be 35 words per minute.[1] You probably read faster than that, otherwise it would have taken you about 33 hours to get to this point in the book, and most people go through *War and Peace, Hawaii, Anna Karenina,* or *The Third Reich* in less time that that.

This implies that either you read by skipping, or alternatively you view groups of letters as single units. Most business executives learn early in their career that they must develop one or the other technique for increasing their reading speed.

Ronald Carver reports that the average freshman is reading at a rate of 300 words per minute, and frequently, at the time he or she graduates the reading speed has increased to over 600 words per minute.[2] According to Carver, there is reason to believe that this efficiency has been developed less by reading clusters of words than by learning to skip. In fact, he points out that we are all physically limited from reading at rates greater than 600 words per minute. Therefore, insofar as higher rates are attained, we must assume that a certain amount of skipping is involved. This phenomenon must be anticipated by the writer. Since you cannot hope to change people's reading habits, you must adjust your written communications so as to ensure that no important part of your message will be lost.

Many executives who have taken a speed-reading course think

that even when they skip, they are collecting all the important information. These people may be the victims of a speed-reading ruse. It appears that some of the foremost speed-reading instructors trick their students by coordinating reading lessons and tests. For example, they may teach that the central idea is contained in the first sentence, with the rest being unimportant. By using appropriate tests that measure the comprehension of the first sentences of the test material, the instructor is able to fool the pupils into thinking that this technique works. They count all the words in the paragraph, contrast them with their high scores, and conclude that they can skip 90 percent of the material and still be 90 percent effective—forgetting that there may be a great difference between the material on which they were tested and the communications with which they have to deal in everyday life.

Unfortunately, industry has subjected many of us to courses of this type, and we have come to think that we can skip over the treasured words recorded by our colleagues. In fact, the amount of reading required from a manager is growing to such an extent that many people are truly unable to read full reports without neglecting their other responsibilities. In short, there can be no doubt that a popular technique among managers is to skip over written reports. Consequently, just because you have written something and addressed it to a specific person, do not assume that your entire message has been received.

The psychological differences between readers and writers make the chore of effective writing particularly difficult. Saul Gellerman lists some reasons why people write when other communication channels are available.[3] It appears that people who choose the written medium over other forms of communication do so to satisfy needs that have nothing to do with communication. According to Gellerman, they write because (1) they receive various forms of applause from writing; (2) writing yields an unusual channel of distinction that is relatively unobstructed by competition; and (3) they enjoy saying something well.

When you contrast these reasons for writing with the motivations for reading, it is no wonder that the average reader is induced to skip. As a reader, you are interested in the one aspect—information—that may be least on the writer's mind.

The first thing to consider before you sit down to compose a memo, then, is what the purpose of your communication is. Are you trying to give essential information? If not, don't waste your own time and that of your readers; they will be quick to learn that you are a memo addict and altogether stop reading what comes from your desk.

But let us suppose that you do have an important message. Why put it in writing? Too often, we simply don't stop to ask that question. The widespread habit of communicating through memos not only depersonalizes relations but also prevents rapid feedback, which is an essential prerequisite of resonance. If you can say it, say it; you save yourself a lot of energy that is better applied to other tasks, and your associates will be grateful to you for not taking their time unnecessarily.

Still, let us assume that what you have to say must be put in writing. Perhaps you are working on your quarterly report, or you need to document the fact that you have taken action on a particular problem. Knowing that large parts of what you write will be skipped, how can you make sure that your central message will be received?

In essence, what is needed is a method of "outpsyching the corporate reader"—that is, of overcoming his natural laziness. Some basic elements of this technique are discussed below.

Writing techniques

The key to good writing is to keep in mind the situation of your readers. They have limited time to spend on extracting your message, and it is your responsibility to make their task easier. This can be done in two ways: (1) by structuring your report or memo in such a way that important information is immediately recognizable as such, and (2) by making reading a pleasant experience. The first point relates to the formal organization of your writing, the second primarily to style.

Putting important information where it can be seen. As we discussed earlier in this chapter, people are taught to expect important information in the *beginning* of a communication. Therefore, don't ramble on, or your readers will lose patience. Get to the point in the first paragraph and reserve lengthy details and explanations for later.

In the typical memorandum, this rule holds in two ways. First, the purpose of the memo should be stated clearly and succinctly in the "Subject" line. Secondly, the main point of your communication should be taken up in the first sentence.

In a longer report dealing with a complex subject, it is often not feasible to give all the important information in one sentence or even one paragraph. For instance, if you are describing the research activities for several fundamentally different projects, it is unlikely that you will be able to summarize all the important results in the first paragraph of the report. Still, the rule holds for each chapter or section. You cannot expect a busy executive to read on to the end of each chapter to find out what went on in the research laboratories.

Of course, even if you stuck with this rule, there will be information in the body of the text that you consider relatively important. Short of being able to put it in the first paragraph, you must find other ways of drawing attention to it.

There are several attention-getting devices that can be used under such circumstances. The golden rule with all of them, however, is to use them sparingly: The more things you draw attention to, the greater the chance that none of them will be noticed. In my experience, no more than 10 percent of the information in most documents is truly important; the rest is support information and should not be highlighted.

The simplest device for highlighting material internal to a text is *underlining* or, alternatively, the use of italics. Ideally, the reader should be able to glean the important message of your report or memo by simply following the underlined material. The following example illustrates this technique.

Major competitors in this business are those of the size of A, B, or C, where research and development in optics design and processing are vital to the support of in-house products, copiers, and microfilm readers and reader-printers. Manufacturing facilities are generally highly mechanized, and tooling is sophisticated. Major emphasis in these companies is on design and well-coordinated engineering to meet high product-quality standards.

Total employment at each of these companies exceeds 10,000, but a good estimate would be that less than 2,000 employees are engaged in optics-related activities.

Intermediate competitors with annual sales volumes of $1 million to $5 million in the optics product area include X, Y, and Z. These companies have limited R&D capabilities, frequently use consultants for optical design work, and do little process development. Most manufacturing equipment is fairly conventional. These firms differ in their efficiency and areas of expertise. Employment in these companies is less than 200.

Small competitors with less than $1 million annual sales volume in the optics product area include the Japanese shops with no prime products. These companies do only contract customer work. Optics processing is often done in a "cottage industry" fashion, using individuals who work independently. Details of the available technology and production capabilities are sketchy at this time, but from our recent visits to the orient, it appears that these companies lack sophistication in many assembly areas. On the other hand, they enjoy low overhead and constitute formidable competition on simple precision jobs.

The use of *headlines* is another way of focusing the reader's attention on important points. For instance, our last example might be reworked along the following lines.

MAJOR COMPETITORS

These are businesses of the size of A, B, or C, where research and development are vital to the support of in-house products. . . .

TECHNOLOGY

Manufacturing facilities are generally highly mechanized, and tooling is sophisticated. . . .

EMPLOYMENT

Total employment in each of these companies exceeds 10,000, but a good estimate would be that less than 2,000 employees are engaged in optics-related activities.

INTERMEDIATE COMPETITORS

These are businesses like X, Y, or Z, which have annual sales volumes of $1 million to $5 million.

TECHNOLOGY

Companies in this category have limited R&D capabilities. They frequently use consultants for optical design work and do little process development. . . .

EMPLOYMENT

Employment in these companies is less than 200 employees.

SMALL COMPETITORS

These are businesses with annual sales volumes of less than $1 million. This category includes the Japanese shops with no prime products. . . .

TECHNOLOGY

Details of the available technology and production capabilities are sketchy at this time, but. . . .

EMPLOYMENT

Optics processing is often done in a "cottage industry" fashion. . . .
Consequently, these companies enjoy low overhead and constitute formidable competition on simple precision jobs.

Finally, we can use *spacing* and various *itemizers* (such as dash-
es) to highlight our important points. If we opted for that solution, our example might take the following shape.

Our competitors in the optics area fall into three categories:

—Major competitors with annual sales exceeding $5 million.
—Intermediate competitors with annual sales volumes of $1 million
to $5 million.
—Small competitors with annual sales of less than $1 million.

Major competitors include A, B, C, and companies of similar size. Examples of intermediate competitors are X, Y, and Z. Small competitors
include the Japanese shops without prime products. The key factors to
be considered in our competition are *technology* and *employment:*

—Major competitors have highly mechanized manufacturing facilities
and sophisticated tooling. Employment exceeds 10,000 for any of
these companies, but a good estimate would be that less than 2,000
employees are engaged in optics-related activities.
—Intermediate competitors have limited R&D capabilities,
frequently use consultants for optical work, and do little process
development. . . . Employment is generally less than 200.
—Small competitors often do optics processing in "cottage industry"
fashion. . . .

If you have followed the advice given so far, you will have
helped your readers by putting important information where they
can readily spot it. Yet, they may fall asleep after the second page
of your report or the second paragraph of your memo. What is
wrong with what you have written?

Chances are it is simply boring. Now, there's no reason why
corporate communications should be dull, long-winded, or pomp-
ous. Give your associates a break and take the drudgery out of
reading. Here are some hints that may prove useful.

Start with a strong lead. Your readers are probably tired by the
time they get around to reading your memo. The telephone has
been ringing all day, and the boss has been on their backs to get
that report in. Wake them up with your first sentence.

Here are the beginnings of two memos about the same subject.
Which one is more likely to make you want to read on?

While it is not the company's policy to interfere with people's personal tastes, circumstances have arisen that make it necessary once more to point out the importance of the image projected by our offices to the success of our business. In the recent past, it has been noticed by several officers as well as outsiders that many offices gave an untidy impression and that in some cases the decor was inappropriate. . . .

Does the state of your office suggest that the last hurricane played havoc with your files or that a bunch of teenagers decorated your walls with their left-over posters? There is no reason why our offices should look as if no work is done in them, and something less than original Rembrandts will do for your walls. However, please keep in mind that clients who visit headquarters *look* at it. The impression of our company that they take home will not be improved by untidy or carelessly decorated offices. . . .

Our point about leads also applies to the "Subject" line of a memorandum. Remember that the conventional form of the memo is by no means God-given. Unless your company is a conservative outfit that frowns upon junior executives who break golden traditions, you might consider the occasional use of an eye-catching headline instead of the usual dry Subject line. Judge for yourself which interdepartmental memo is most likely to be read:

To: J.C. Henry
From: S. VanDer Slice
Subject: 4324 Department—Manufacturing Yields

To: J.C. Henry
From: S. VanDer Slice
Subject: The Hen That Laid a Golden Egg

Once again, before you strike out with such experimental variations of the traditional memo, make sure that your company is the right place to do it. And whatever you do, be circumspect; you never know who might be reading what you put on paper. One thing you should *never* do, no matter how clever it seems at the time, is to make a joke at somebody else's expense. Nobody will respect you for it, and the victim of your joke will take the next opportunity to pay you back in kind.

Use strong, active words. Passive expressions like "it has been decided" or "it was concluded" serve only to hide the identities of whoever was responsible for the decision or the conclusion. If you find yourself using passive forms to excess, ask yourself why you are doing it. Are you afraid to take responsibility? That implies that you are not sure you did the right thing. Or are you trying to sound more important than you are? The reader won't buy it.

Avoid long or unfamiliar words. Why write "hypothesize" if "believe" or "assume" will do? Don't turn out memos that have to be read with *Webster's Third New International Dictionary* on the side. Chances are the reader won't consult the dictionary but simply throw your memo into the wastebasket.

People use big words because (1) they're too lazy to think of short ones that will do the job as well or better; (2) they're not sure of what they want to say in the first place; or (3) they want to impress somebody as sophisticated.

Use short sentences. If you can't read a sentence in your memo without taking a breath or two, you're on the wrong track. Keep your sentences to a maximum of about 20 words. In most cases, 10 to 15 words will be best. Compare the following two examples and decide for yourself which is easier to read.

> Due to increases in the costs of labor, utilities, supplies, and federal as well as local taxes, only partly offset by increased productivity in our manufacturing operations, the operating costs of our division have risen sharply, by 12 percent, or $2 million, calling for an extensive reevaluation of all operations, whether staff or line, possibly using a zero-base approach.

> Operating costs for our division were up sharply by $2 million, or 12 percent. This reflects increased costs of labor, utilities, supplies, and federal and local taxes. The cost increases were only partly offset by increased productivity in our manufacturing operations. To reverse this trend, we will reevaluate all staff and line operations, possibly using a zero-base approach.

Use short paragraphs. Does your memo look like an excerpt from a stream-of-consciousness novel, with single paragraphs spanning one or more pages? What may be fine for fiction writing isn't fine for business communications. Mark new thoughts by starting new paragraphs; in general, they should not exceed five to six lines.

Again, the first sentence of each paragraph should carry the main thought. The rest is reserved for supporting material that may be skipped if necessary. Occasionally, you may feel that a thought spans more than six lines. But even in such cases, it is usually possible to divide the material into several paragraphs.

Prepare for bad news by giving good news first. This is a matter less of style than of psychology. Nobody likes bad news, but if you must give it, at least compensate by saying something pleasant first. You don't want to be known as a messenger of corporate doom.

End on a positive note. Just as you should ease into bad news, you want to close in such a way that you will be remembered as someone who looks at the positive side of things. When your readers put down your memo or report, they should feel that there is some hope that things will turn out all right.

Be modest. Do all of your sentences start with "I"? This will be taken as an indication that you think mostly about yourself. Show that there are some other things that you're concerned about. If you practice this long enough in your writing, it might even genuinely change your outlook—and make you a better manager.

Reread what you have written. First of all, check that you got all names and titles correct. People do not take lightly to seeing their names mutilated or in three different versions. Also, if you are not sure about the spelling of a word, consult the dictionary. But most important, check that the tone is right and that your message comes across clearly.

Put yourself in the position of your reader, who may be pressed for time and know little about things that you tend to take for granted. Is all the important information in the right places and properly highlighted? Are your paragraphs manageable? Have you left any unfamiliar abbreviations? And finally, would you want to read past the first sentence if the piece were addressed to you? Be hard on yourself; it will pay off.

"If I Say It, They Will Hear It"

Just as you should keep in mind that what you write may not be read, you should not assume that what you say will necessarily be heard and absorbed. There are two factors that you have to consider here: (1) your efficiency as a speaker, and (2) various conditions that turn people into bad listeners. Both factors, I believe, are at least partly under your control. This is more obvious in the case of the first factor, which will be discussed in detail in a later section, but it also holds for the second point.

What makes people bad listeners is their mental state. For one thing, they may be distracted and simply not pay attention to what you say; for another, they may be prevented from getting your message by a strong bias that lets them hear only what they want to hear.

The effect of bias on people's perceptions is well illustrated by two experiments. In an experiment by Seymour Feshback and Robert Singer, a group of people were subjected to an electrical shock while they were asked to watch a motion picture showing two people interacting.[4] The group was then divided, and one half was allowed to talk about the shock, whereas the other half was not allowed to discuss it. Subsequently, both halves were questioned about their impressions of the picture.

The subjects who were not allowed to discuss the shock interpreted the actions of the principal actor as more negative than the subjects who were allowed to talk about their experience. The most surprising result of this experiment, however, was that the subjects who developed a more negative impression were not aware of the subconscious influence that contributed to their thinking.

Loren Wispé, and Nicholas Drambarean showed a similar kind of bias effect in a group of people whom they subjected to starvation.[5] The group was starved for about 24 hours. After ten hours, the subjects were tested. It was found that the recognition time for need words like *food* and *drink* was faster than in a control group responding to nonneed words. In other words, it appeared that after ten hours of starving, people had become more perceptive for words that had to do with their immediate needs.

This bias effect is just as one might have expected. However, it was also noticed that after the group was starved for 24 hours, the recognition time for need words had gone up from hundredths of a second to sometimes almost a full second. What this reversal seems to indicate is that when deprivation becomes extreme, people unwittingly suppress recognition of the needs. In other words, we can interpret subjects' difficulties in recognizing food words after this period as caused by a protective mechanism that shuts off perceptions that might cause anxiety.

The results of these studies have direct application to the business situation. Consider what we have learned from the experiments. First, we have seen that bias tends to distort people's perceptions. If you have an acute need to be recognized for your work, for instance, you will be "primed" to discern any sign of appreciation. At the same time, you may be inclined to ignore any remark that implies a criticism of your performance. On the other hand, if your need for recognition has taken on such proportions that it causes you severe anxiety, you may actually block the perception of anything that even remotely bears on the subject of your anxiety, whether it is praise or criticism.

As a manager, you must keep in mind that such bias may exist in your listeners. Again, if you do not take the trouble to find out what is uppermost on your associates' minds, you will be unable to anticipate and counteract listener bias. You may think that you have said clearly what you wanted to say—only to find out that your colleague or subordinate understood you to say the opposite.

Secondly, we have seen that discussion tends to help remove bias. In practical terms, if you know that a man on your staff is worried about his wife, who is in the hospital after an accident, you would be ill advised to talk to him about production yields without first discussing the one thing that causes him anxiety. Even though he may not be aware of it, his interpretation of what you say will probably be colored by his worries.

Before discussing some techniques for reducing listener bias, let me remark briefly on your own role as a listener.

Clearly, there are times when you do not wish to interrupt the speaker, yet as he or she talks, certain ideas might occur to you that you are anxious not to forget. I have found that when this happens, my objectivity as a listener suffers because my attention is taken by the points that I wish to remember.

In order to eliminate this undue influence, I have developed a technique that I find at least partially successful. As an idea occurs to me while I am listening, I jot down a brief reminder and put the sheet in my "in" basket. This, I find, enables me to forget about it and to listen with a clean, uncluttered mind.

You may find that a similar technique works in your own case. In any event, you must take steps to prevent bias from coloring your perceptions, just as you must make sure that your listeners are receptive to what you have to say.

There are also some specific exercises that you might consider in order to improve your listening skills.

For instance, sit in a relaxed position in a quiet room and try to hear the faint noise of a refrigerator or an air conditioner, or noises outside. With enough practice, you should be able to hear your own heartbeat. Five minutes of this practice each day should be sufficient. In addition to sharpening your sensitivity to sounds, this exercise will help you relax and even control your own mind.

Turning to comprehension skills, there are numerous effective training programs, such as the audio-tape program marketed by Basic Systems, Inc. This particular program, which has been proven effective at the college level, develops listening skills by presenting the student with progressively longer and more complex statements, followed by content questions. Students are allowed to compare their answers with the solutions in the program manual. Furthermore, there are brief instructions for effective listening interspersed between the exercises.

If you do not wish to use such commercially marketed programs, you might consider developing your own exercises. A useful procedure is to make written outlines of presentations or discussions. Alternatively, you might mentally summarize your impression of what you just heard.

Clearly, the most basic aspect of comprehension is memory. There are a multitude of exercises and techniques for improving your ability at recall, including such simple games as "In my suitcase I have a . . ." In this children's game, each person repeats the sentence, adding another noun; the winner is the one who can remember the longest series of nouns.

Another exercise, which does not require other participants, involves trying to remember the series of mental images that occurred to you over a period of five or ten minutes. As you continue this exercise, you will be amazed at the number of images that you are able to recall.

Putting your listeners in a receptive mood

Some of the rules that we are about to discuss may seem so elementary to you that you wonder how anybody could overlook them. Yet, it is amazing how often they are ignored, even by people who would be quick to recognize the same mistakes in others. To be biased, your listeners do not need to be preoccupied with problems of cosmic dimensions. Little things you say or do may be sufficient to turn them off and make them miss your message.

Make your listeners comfortable. Nobody likes to listen standing up, sharing a chair with your briefcase, or looking at you across a foot-high pile of papers. It indicates lack of respect for the other person and is likely to produce a resentment that will influence what the listener hears. By the same token, don't doodle, fiddle, or groom yourself while talking. The listener is more likely to think about your lack of courtesy than about what you are saying.

Make a habit of studying your listener's reactions. If his face indicates that he's falling asleep or thinking about something else, do something to gain his attention back. If you detect signs of disapproval or annoyance, don't simply go on. Find out why he reacts the way he does. Ask him if he disagrees with you or why he seems disturbed. It only costs you a minute, and it may save hours.

Don't unnecessarily correct minor mistakes. If you have a major problem to discuss, set the stage with some positive remarks and get to the point. Don't create unnecessary antagonism by dispensing criticism for minor mistakes that can be taken care of at a later time. If you do, chances are the listener will turn off by the time you get to the real problem.

Don't hesitate to pay compliments. Again, this sets the stage and helps put your listener in a receptive mood. Everybody welcomes good news, so if there is any, give it. It will go a long way toward getting your listener's cooperation on problems that must be solved.

On the other hand, don't overdo this. If you have to discuss something disagreeable, don't spend half an hour saying nice things. For one thing, it will sound insincere in retrospect. For another, you will have created the wrong atmosphere, and the bad news will come as a shock, or its importance will be lost on the listener. As always, you must exercise your own judgment here.

Consider your face and body while you talk. We will discuss this issue in greater detail in the next chapter. For the moment, just keep in mind that your facial expressions and your "body language" should go along with what you say. The listener will be puzzled if you make critical remarks with a broad grin or give good news while banging your fist on the desk or holding a lecturing finger up. Generally, avoid anything that would tend to distract the listener or make him doubt that you mean what you say.

Know your listeners and what is on their minds. This has already been mentioned, but it bears repeating here, for it is the most fundamental rule of synergistic management. Unless you are blessed with extraordinary psychological intuitions, you cannot anticipate how people will react to what you say if you don't know more about them than their names. As we all know, some people are less receptive or more preoccupied with problems than others and therefore may need to be more carefully prepared if they are to get your message. Take an interest; the results will be rewarding.

"If I Put It in Writing, There Will Be No Ambiguity"

The third false assumption is that you can avoid ambiguity by putting things in writing. But as our discussion of listener bias should have made clear, people tend to hear only what they want to hear, and there is no reason to believe that this does not hold for reading as well.

There are two major cases in which people use writing to avoid ambiguity. The first is obvious: it is the contract. People write contracts so that all sources of possible misunderstanding can be eliminated. The second is the corporate memo or some variation thereof. The memo writer frequently writes in order to have a record that he or she asked for something or took a specific action.

More commonly, however, memos are written simply because there is no trust. This attitude may be appropriate for a contract, but it is out of place for ordinary corporate communications. In fact, it only serves to strengthen the atmosphere of mistrust—besides failing to eliminate ambiguities.

In the case of a contract, we can to some extent rely on the professional lawyer to compose a piece without ambiguities. The lawyer's tools include special training and court-tested phrases. Yet, in spite of this, other lawyers are often able to find a second way to interpret the language in the contract. In view of this, you cannot possibly hope to write a memo that is not open to misinterpretation. Instead, it is usually better to talk, for this gives both parties an opportunity to ask questions and thereby reduces the amount of misunderstanding.

As a standard procedure, then, I recommend to ask for things in a personal conversation. When I do this with people whom I do not know, I keep track of my person-to-person request with a note to myself, which is put in my follow-up files. If no response occurs, I make a second or third or fourth request and insert this in the same file. After the third request, I may send a copy of my personal reminder with all the follow-up dates to the person in question, with a personal note like "How about it?" This almost always brings results.

The one thing you should never do—and unfortunately, this is a popular procedure—is to send copies of your memo to chains of people, including the superior of the addressee. This amounts to an open declaration of mistrust and is the surest way of creating bad feelings. If you want to write to the boss, write directly to him.

Although most writing is done because there is a lack of trust, there are cases when you can actually *create* trust by writing. I put in writing what I said or promised to do, not what the other person agreed to do. In this respect, statements like "I will give you back-up information prior to July 22" are commendable and preferable to things like "We agree" or "You promised to give me your full report by July 25." Clearly, it is easier for others to trust you when they have a gun in their hand. To establish trust, somebody has to take the first step, and giving others a potential weapon against you can do wonders to further your cause.

When writing must be used, I make an effort to keep the messages as personal as possible. In essence, it should be a shared secret between the receiver and myself. In that spirit, I prefer hand-written notes to the formality of typed communications. This has the additional advantage of assuring the receiver that the information passed on to him is confidential and has not been shared with your secretary. Admittedly, this is not always essential, but there may well be cases where this can make a difference and allow for frankness that would otherwise be impossible.

In general, however, keep in mind that besides adding to the trust barrier, written communications serve to slow down feedback. It is wrong to assume that a written note should be answered with a written note. That is valid only when trust is missing and you fear that the lack of writing can be used as a weapon against you. Usually, it is far better to take the memo in hand and visit its originator. Respond to the request in conversation and then forget it—you will probably have cut off two or three days of ineffective message transmission, besides having increased the chances for trust and resonance.

"Our Communicative Habits Cannot Be Changed"

The assumption that you cannot improve your communication skills is tied to a whole series of popular misconceptions. For example, the ability to listen is not, as some people seem to believe, strongly correlated to your basic ability to hear.[6] Also, you are not a born introvert, and you do not talk in a monotone because that is "you." Probably you talk the way you do because you have developed habits that have been cultivated from childhood, and because of their deep-rooted nature they are particularly difficult to break.

I believe that you can train your mind not to wander while reading or listening; that you can improve your memory; that you can learn to read faster or write better; and that you can learn to make conversation like Barbara Walters.

Increasing Your Efficiency as a Speaker

We have already discussed some techniques for increasing your efficiency as a listener, as well as various ways to fight listener bias. The latter are, in a sense, part of your skills as a speaker, because they help you get your message across. Here, we will deal with techniques that are more obviously related to speaking.

Make sure your listeners are ready for what you have to say. First of all, communication is easier in a relaxed state. Give some thought to seating and lighting. You are not trying to "grill" your listeners, so make them comfortable. Secondly, keep in mind that people need some "warm-up" time. If you feel it might be necessary, spend a minute or two on general talk, then get to your points.

Introduce your subject clearly. You may think that people come to the meeting armed with the same information as you. More often than not, they do not have the same preparation as you. Make sure you state clearly what your purpose is and explain all basic facts and assumptions before elaborating or drawing conclusions.

If you are a production manager, and the controller or a lawyer attends one of your meetings, don't jump into an intricate technical discussion. Chances are this person knows little about what is going on in the mills, and your speech will be lost on him or her. You will do everybody a good service by starting with a brief review of the operations or problems you are about to discuss.

Control your volume. In general, you should talk loudly. Not only does it make listening easier, it also prevents people from letting their attention slip. Nothing sends people to sleep more easily than a speaker who is mumbling into his beard. Furthermore, if you speak too softly, people will get the impression that you are not enthusiastic about your subject.

There is a subtler aspect to this. Maxwell Maltz has noted that by speaking loudly, the speaker himself derives additional stimulation and may be able to overcome inhibitions.[7] In fact, he proposed speaking loudly as a method for changing one's personality type from introvert to extrovert. Therefore, if you know yourself to tend toward shyness, you should make a special effort to keep your volume at a higher level than you would naturally select.

Of course, this works in the opposite way too. One might well try to persuade extreme extroverts to lower their speaking volume in order to reduce their contributions to a more reasonable level.

Even if you followed this advice, however, your presentation may be ineffective because it is monotonous. Controlling your volume means more than just talking loudly, it implies deliberate *variation.*

As a rule, the volume of your speech should be related to the relative importance of what you are saying. Just as you will underline the important parts of a memo or report, so you should give prominence to your critical points by raising your volume. By doing this, you are giving your listeners an effective guide to interpreting your presentation.

Control your speed. The average rate of speaking is about 120 words per minute. This rate should be varied according to the content of what you have to say. In particular, you should remember that ordinarily, you will give new as well as familiar information. Because processing new information requires a greater mental effort, you should give the listener extra time. In other words, you should speak more slowly when introducing new concepts or facts.

On the other hand, people are apt to get restless if you dwell on points that are familiar to them. Although you will often need to summarize old information, you can forestall boredom by increasing your speaking rate during such passages.

Help your listeners remember your important points. This calls for periodic summaries. Unlike in the case of written material, your listeners cannot go back over what you said. Instead, they must rely on you to provide a healthy amount of repetition. Don't talk as if your audience were composed of a bunch of computers that do not know the meaning of the word "forget."

Pace your presentation. Moray conducted an experiment that indicates that people are unable to shift attention to new signals of the simplest kind more than four times a second.[8] Considering the complexity of the subjects discussed in a typical business meeting, you must assume that your listeners need some time to get ready for a new topic. Therefore, break up your presentation, if necessary, with short periods of rest or humorous anecdotes.

If appropriate, offer visual aids. Slides, flip charts, mimeographed summaries, or the blackboard may be helpful to illustrate your point in a simple, concise way. Don't overdo this, however. People may miss your next point because they are enjoying themselves looking at your graphics.

In addition, practice the techniques discussed earlier for effective writing. In particular, use short, simple, active words and short sentences, break between new thoughts, and start and end on a positive note.

Mental Practice

In the following, I describe two exercises that you can do in the privacy of your home or in your car as you drive to work. They have proved helpful in my own case, but obviously, there is no reason to think that my inadequacies are the same as yours. Therefore, you may well want to invent your own exercises that meet your specific needs better.

Practice shouting

It is said that the Greek orator Demosthenes tried to improve the volume of his speaking voice by walking along the seashore on rough days and outshouting the wind and the waves. You may not feel the urge to join Demosthenes' ranks, but if you tend to speak too softly, you may find practice shouting a useful exercise. This is best done in the privacy of your own car—with the windows closed, unless you want to invite strange looks from other drivers or pedestrians. Two or three minutes of this exercise each day should be sufficient.

I took up this exercise several years ago when I was lost and pulled up beside a man who was mowing his lawn. He kept asking "What?" and I kept on repeating my request for directions louder and louder. In the end, he had to turn off his lawn mower in order to understand me.

I realized that I was not physiologically limited from shouting. Instead, there seemed to be some psychological barrier that would not let me raise my voice above a certain level. I decided it was time to correct this attitude.

Of course, I am not suggesting that you should manage by shouting. Quite to the contrary; the less shouting you do, the better. However, the exercise, awkward as it may seem at first, may help you develop a habit of speaking more loudly and forcefully.

Practice conversation

To some, keeping a conversation rolling comes easy; to others, it is a major mental effort. If you are the latter type, you may find the exercise described here useful.

To practice conversation with a good conversationalist requires no particular skill, because he or she will provide you with all the cues you need. To converse efficiently with a poor speaker, on the other hand, is quite a different matter. This is where talking to yourself—assuming that your conversational skills are somewhat less than brilliant—is a valuable exercise. Surely, if you are able to maintain an interesting monolog, you should find it easy to carry on a dialog with anybody.

Most people probably recall being chided as children for talking to themselves. You may remember the saying that people who talk to themselves have money in the bank. Although I cannot promise you that playing the conversation game will give your bank account a boost, I wouldn't be surprised if in fact this happened.

Any subject will do for this exercise—life after death, the feelings of plants, the value of exercise or dieting, or new products that could be used in your business. The most remarkable thing about practicing conversation, I found, is the clarity of the ideas that you develop. Talking out loud, in my experience, helps shut out external stimuli and maintain a focus on your subject that is missing in simple nonverbalized thinking. In short, this game may improve not only your conversational skills but also your creativity.

In my own case, I noticed that after a while of playing this game, I began to repeat myself. At this point I realized that I needed additional external stimulation, and I began sharing my ideas with my colleagues. You may find that in order to maintain a flow of fresh ideas, you have to do the same.

In fact, there is no reason to believe that you should practice conversation only by yourself. There will be numerous occasions—be it at work, with friends, or at cocktail parties—where you can test and develop your conversational skills. Just start the ball rolling and watch for the cues as they emerge.

The best way to look at our conversation exercise, as the foregoing discussion implies, is as a game. If you think back over the games you played, you will find that they have three characteristics in common: (1) a name, (2) an objective, and (3) rules.

A good name for our conversation game would be "Talk and Listen." This is what participants should do in conversations. Unfortunately, people too often seem to forget about the second part of the game. They develop an irrational fear of silence, and instead of listening, they merely think about what they will say next.

Ironically, because in this way they deprive themselves of the stimuli from their conversation partners, the dialog usually dies down anyhow. To have a successful conversation, then, you must keep alert to the cues provided by the other person.

To get a view of the objectives of this game, consider briefly the purpose of playing a game like basketball or tennis. The most obvious objective—and to some people, it seems, the only one—is to win the game. As some people are fond of stating: "Winning isn't everything; it's the only thing."

A moment's reflection will make it clear that this is exactly the way many people approach a conversation: They want to drive a point home or outwit their "opponent." If they do not succeed in this, they seem to feel that they've wasted their time.

A good conversation should be compared not to a competitive

but to a *cooperative* game. Olive Heseltine captured this spirit in her book *Conversation:*

> Conversation is . . . like a game of battledore and shuttlecock, where each player may strike in at his will, but the shuttlecock must never be allowed to fall to the ground.
>
> The qualities most necessary to a good game are quickness and lightness, a background of culture and a common idiom, a general familiarity with the topics chosen and a readiness on the part of all to allow each player his turn.[9]

One of the major objectives of the game, then, is to keep the "shuttlecock" in the air, and rather than trying to outwit the other players, you should attempt to place your shots so that they can be returned.

As with sports games, however, a second objective is simply to exercise your skills. The proficient tennis player will have improved his hand-and-eye coordination, increased his speed of reaction, and trained his body. Similarly, practicing conversation may increase your sensitivity to cues, improve your reactions to unanticipated responses, and generally train your mind. In short, it may help you develop the skills that are essential for successful social interactions and creative conflict resolution.

Finally, the rules of the game prescribe how it is to be set in motion, how it continues once it has begun, and what moves are allowed to change the course of the game. It is amusing how we can think for hours about our wardrobe, yet we spend almost no time thinking about what we will say in a conversation. Somehow our wardrobe is something that we feel needs proper preparation, yet for our mental dress we feel no responsibility.

Most of us would never admit to calculating conversation, and some of us will not admit to premeditated speeches. It is almost socially unacceptable to give thought to how we will promote our conversation, or, more specifically, what we will say after we say "hello." Yet, I believe that some thought should be given to how to start and maintain a fruitful conversation.

Admittedly, this can be carried to extremes. I have recently heard of an executive who has a series of prepared discussions. He and his wife both study subjects that they wish to discuss. They make notes, prepare statements, and then practice conversing the particular subject that they have studied. They have a series of these subjects which they have prepared over the years.

When they are out for the evening, they start a discussion of a topic that they suspect will be interesting to their company. They are prepared mentally, and they frequently receive ideas that they can add to their standard presentations.

Perhaps you consider this game too extreme; I do too, but nevertheless, it is an excellent example of the mechanics of the conversation game. If I were to criticize this variation of the game, it would be on the basis not of overpreparation but of inflexibility. In other words, practicing conversation should not go so far as to leave no room for listening to the other person with an open mind.

Conversation openers. The game can be started with either a question or a statement. You can consider your move successful if it "struck a cord" with the respondent—in other words, if you achieved a certain degree of resonance.

Your opener should be neither overused ("Nice day, isn't it?") nor too general ("How are things going with you?"). Brilliant conversationalists will use openers that allow them to learn more about the other person's background. To take a simple example, "Isn't it a nice day?" may lead to no more than a routine answer ("It sure is"), whereas "This is the kind of day I would like to be out playing golf" is likely to elicit a thought-out response that will at least tell you whether the other person is interested in golf or what his or her other hobbies are.

As the example suggests, to initiate a conversation, you generally have to tell something about yourself first. In a sense, this is trivial, for anything we say discloses some information about ourselves. The point, of course, is to select information that has some relation to the other person's own realm of experience, and this is not always easy, especially when you have little knowledge about your conversation partners.

Try playing the game with topics that can be expected to hold some general interest—major news items, a situation in the office, principles that seem to govern people's behavior, or problems you observe as your children grow up. Then put yourself in the situation of somebody you know and "watch" as the conversation develops.

Conversation in motion. Once the conversation is off to a good start, the objective is to keep the ball rolling. The secret, as we discussed before, is not merely to add new stimuli but to respond to the cues offered by the other person. Furthermore, each contribution should be kept to a reasonable length so as to allow the listener to respond intelligently. Keep in mind that one of your objectives in this cooperative game is to make the other person feel good; both partners should emerge with the feeling that they have won.

At this stage, you can practice much more than just your conversational skills. You can test yourself and find out how much— or how little—you really know about your associates. In fact, after speculating, in your game, how a particular person might respond to your questions and statements, you may want to compare his or her imagined responses with the real thing. Chances are you will find that the image you have formed falls short of reality. In the end, you will have learned something important about your friends, colleagues, or subordinates.

Apart from practicing your control of volume, speed, inflection, and nonverbals, you can also use this opportunity to improve your "editing" function. As you prepare to speak, consider the impact of what you are about to say on the other person. Are there any ambiguities left that might lead to misunderstandings? In what light will your contribution appear to the other person? Again, to answer these questions, you have to know how your friends or associates think and feel, what their problems and peculiarities are.

A last point about keeping a conversation moving: Statements modified by subjective expressions like "I believe" or "I think" tend to be more provocative than simple assertions of facts. When we say, "I believe," we imply, "Please tell me if you agree or disagree with me." To put it differently, it indicates that we expect a response and that we are willing to consider it seriously. It may mean the difference between an argument and a conversation.

Conclusion

In summary, we have seen in this chapter that there are several faulty assumptions about verbal skills that may create misunderstandings and affect the manager's effectiveness as a communicator.

One, people may not read what you write. You must antici-pate this and take steps to ensure that your message will not be lost or distorted.

Two, people may not listen to what you say. Again, you can avoid problems by making sure that your listeners are in a state to receive your message, and you can also increase your chances of being heard by improving your skills as a speaker.

Three, the mere act of putting something in writing does not avoid ambiguities. Frequently, you will be better off relying on face-to-face conversations, where feedback can be used to elimi-nate misunderstandings. Also, this will speed up the exchange of information, and clearly, nobody benefits from delays in corporate communications.

Finally, it is not true that we cannot change our com-munication habits. As I have tried to show, we can train ourselves to become better listeners, to write better letters, memos, or re-ports, and to speak more efficiently. The key, as with all success-ful interactions, is to put yourself in the situation of the other per-son. If you can master that art, communication will become a fruitful two-way process rather than a dead-end street.

NOTES

1. Kolers, Paul A., "Experiments in Reading," *Scientific American*, July 1972, p. 84.
2. Carver, Ronald P., "Speed Readers Don't Read; They Skim," *Psychology Today*, August 1972, pp. 22–30.
3. Gellerman, Saul. W., *People Problems and Profits*, New York: Mc-Graw-Hill, 1960.
4. Feshback, Seymour, and Robert D. Singer, "The Effects of Fear Arousal and Suppression of Fear Upon Social Perception," *Journal of Abnormal and Social Psychology* 55 (1957), p. 283. As cited in Weaver, C. H., *Human Listening*, New York: Bobbs-Merrill, 1972.
5. Wispé, Loren G., and Nicholas C. Drambarean, "Physiological Need, Word Frequency and Visual Duration Thresholds," *Journal of Experimental Psychology* 46 (1953), p. 25. As cited in Weaver, C. H., *Human Listening*.
6. Bormann, Ernest, William S. Howell, Ralph G. Nichols, and George L. Shapiro, *Interpersonal Communications in the Modern Organi-zation*, Englewood Cliffs, N.J.: Prentice-Hall, 1969.

7. Maltz, Maxwell, *Psycho-Cybernetics*, N. Hollywood, Calif.: Wilshire Book Company, 1960.
8. Moray, N., "Broadbent's Filter Theory: Postulate H and the Problem of Switching Time," *Quarterly Journal of Experimental Psychology* 12 (1960). As cited in Weaver, C. H., *Human Listening*.
9. Heseltine, Olive, *Conversation*, New York: E. P. Dutton & Co., 1927. pp. 1–2.

Nonverbal Communication

8

Everyone who has worked in industry has witnessed the situation where a group of people attend a meeting in order to discuss some problem, only to fall into disorganized debate. In fact, this is so common that people have come not to expect any benefits from a meeting. This feeling is aptly summarized by expressions like "Kill time with a committee" or "The only thing to come out of a meeting is people."

This is not surprising. Whereas a face-to-face conversation makes an orderly discussion possible and provides for adequate feedback lacking in written communications, the typical meeting involves a great number of people with different characteristics, possibly talking at the same time, and it is easy for things to get out of control.

Perhaps you have been fortunate enough to be able to watch a skillful executive at one of these occasions and observe some of the ways in which he or she adds order to such a meeting. Often, this person need not *say* anything to control the meeting; instead, he or she communicates clearly and effectively in a nonverbal way.

The fact is that nonverbal communication can be a powerful

tool to wield your influence. It can be used to control a meeting, achieve respect, gain quiet, grant approval, condemn, or intimidate. By mastering these techniques, you can increase your effectiveness as a manager to a surprising extent.

One reason for the importance of nonverbal communiation is its independence from the auditory channel. This provides for instantaneous feedback and allows you to transmit important messages even while others are speaking.

In verbal communication, you must wait your turn. Clearly, it would not only be bad form but also make for disorganized discussion if you talked before the last speaker has finished. By contrast, you can indicate polite disagreement by shaking your head, without interrupting the speaker. In the same way, a smile or affirmative nod can encourage the speaker to go on.

Most people who master the art of nonverbal communication probably do not even realize that they owe their effectiveness at least partly to this secondary "language." In fact, they may not be aware that they are using nonverbals at all. Our use of nonverbals tends to be subconscious, and few people are able to achieve direct control over it.

This is an exciting revelation, for it indicates that if you are more aware of the use and subtleties of nonverbal communication, you can make yourself a much more effective leader. For one thing, it allows you an increased control over communications, because it gives you a means of simultaneous feedback. For another, it provides an invaluable aid to interpreting people's personalities, feelings, and reactions. And finally, it gives you a method of influencing people's behavior in subtle ways.

Nonverbals can support a conversation in various ways. First, they can function as adjectives, if you will, modifying the meaning of the words they accompany. For instance, you may say "no" with a smile or, alternatively, with a fist slamming down on the table. In the first case, your nonverbal signal modifies the meaning of "no" to indicate polite regret, in the second, angry rejection.

Secondly, nonverbals provide a continuous flow of messages that may be quite independent of the verbalized messages that are running parallel with it. For instance, the posture, gestures, and facial expressions of a speaker may signal messages about the person's changing moods, feelings of insecurity, basic arrogance, and so on. It is all there for you to read—if you only know how.

Finally, the nonverbal expressions of listeners may help you identify their reactions to what you say. By keeping alert to these signals, you can do much to smooth the process of communication.

It is easy to delude oneself into thinking that the contribution of nonverbals to communication is sporadic and altogether negligible, and given this common attitude, it is no wonder that most people do not consider it worthwhile to improve their skills in this respect. In fact, however, authorities on the subject conclude that close to 90 percent of a message is transmitted nonverbally. Therefore, it is essential that you master nonverbal techniques of communication.

If nonverbals are as important as we have claimed, then this points further to the need for face-to-face communication, because obviously, writing or telephone conversations cannot use this additional channel. This has long been recognized by professional salespersons, who will tell you that you must never deliver quotations in writing or over the phone. Smart salespersons know that it is necessary to understand the total reaction of a customer to everything that is said. They watch the eyes and posture of the customer and adjust their negotiation according to the reactions they observe.

When the eye pupils enlarge or the customer spreads his legs comfortably, they know that they can increase the price and ask for stiffer sales terms and conditions. Conversely, if the customer folds his arms tightly across the chest, they might be reluctant to quote a higher price. These gesture and expressions, whether consciously or subconsciously controlled, provide stimuli that can be used to augment the overt communication between two people.

A second reason why professional salespersons will insist on face-to-face meetings, especially when it comes to discussing prices and terms, is that this enables them to use nonverbal communication themselves to influence the customer's thinking in subtle but powerful ways. For instance, I remember forcing myself, during a lengthy negotiation, to frown over a point about which I was actually quite happy. The fortunate result was further compromise to my benefit.

Many companies are aware of this, and they will allow only professional buyers to deal with sales representatives. In fact, in my own case, I remember dealing with a buyer who was accompanied by an engineer. As I was quoting prices, the engineer's face lit up, thereby giving the game away. He simply lacked the control over nonverbals essential to a successful negotiation.

There is another common situation where people naturally seek the added benefits of nonverbal communication. Few people would dream of writing a note to ask for a raise. They ask for it in person. Whether or not they realize this, one of the reasons why they do this is because they feel more secure when they can observe the subconscious reactions of the person to whom the request is addressed. Clearly, asking for a higher salary is a delicate negotiation, and to achieve the best result, you require a maximum of immediate feedback.

Before turning to a detailed discussion of how to use and interpret nonverbals, let me remark briefly on one last point. I said earlier that the flow of nonverbal signals can to a certain extent be independent of the verbally expressed message. This raises the issue of consistency.

A sensitive observer will make a decision as to whether or not to trust a speaker on the basis of the consistency of the verbal message with the nonverbal one. To take a simple-minded example, if you smile while telling me that you are upset, I will have reason to doubt your sincerity. On the other hand, if you frown while telling me the same thing, I would be inclined to believe you.

Of course, things are not that simple. We respond to a multitude of different gestures, postures, and facial expressions, and consistency is judged by considering a large number of these. Although it may be easy for people to control any one of these signals, they usually cannot control all of them at once, and with a little effort, it is generally possible to derive the true message conveyed by the totality of their nonverbal signals.

The obvious question that arises when you are faced with a discrepancy between a verbal and a nonverbal message is, which one do you believe? Here is where the importance of nonverbals becomes evident, because there seems to be general agreement that nonverbal signals are more reliable than verbal ones.

In this connection, an experiment conducted by Albert Mehrabian and Susan Ferris is of interest.[1] These authors instructed three female speakers to say the word "maybe" with three different intonations communicating liking, neutrality, or dislike toward an imagined addressee. At the same time, photographs were taken of the speakers, showing the corresponding facial expressions of liking, neutrality, or dislike.

When subjects were asked to judge the attitude of the speakers, it became apparent that the contribution of the facial expressions was significantly stronger than that of the vocal inflections. In other words, even where there is consistency between verbal and nonverbal signals, people tend to pay more attention to nonverbals. We might extrapolate from this that if the verbal message is not compatible with the nonverbal expressions, common sense tells us to rely on the latter.

Reading Nonverbals

As we have mentioned, the skill of interpreting nonverbal signals is essential to synergistic management because it helps you adjust your behavior quickly to the reactions of the people with whom you are dealing. You must learn to "read" unexpressed feelings from the way a person sits, gestures, moves his or her face, and uses space and time. When you have perfected your skills at understanding and interpreting these signals, you will find it that much easier to actively use nonverbals in an effective way.

Body language

The habit of slightly rubbing the nose with the index finger is a good first example of body language. It was originally identified as a sign of hostility by Ray Birdwhistell.[2] He identified the nose rub among Americans as a sign of rejection—as a "no." It may also be interpreted as a sign of doubt, or uncertainty. For instance, if it occurs after a question is asked, it may be a clue that the respondent is asking himself whether or not to answer the question at all, that he is not convinced of the validity of what he is about to say, or that he is not sure of the best way to communicate his belief.

You might expect to observe this gesture frequently during a negotiation, especially at the beginning of the meeting. As the negotiating parties come closer to an understanding, the frequency of this gesture will probably decrease. Therefore, it may be used as an indicator of whether or not progress is being achieved.

One might object that this gesture can easily be misread, because people may rub their noses simply to alleviate an itch. However, there is a distinct difference between rubbing the nose when it itches and rubbing it as an expression of doubt or negative feelings. The sensitive observer should have no difficulty distinguishing the two.

Another popular gesture is steepling. This gesture involves joining the fingertips to form what might be described as a church steeple. Steepling connotes a confident, sometimes smug, egotistic, proud attitude. It communicates that the steepler is sure of what he or she is saying and suggests an attitude of absolute self-confidence.

There are several less extreme forms of steepling that a person might subconsciusly adopt so as not to let the degree of his or her self-confidence become evident. These include positioning the fingers on the lap while sitting or joining fingers slightly at belt level when standing. Yet another variation is lightly holding one hand on top of the other as though the church steeple has broken. This is nonarrogant, subdued steepling.

The more important people feel, the higher they will generally hold their hands while steepling. The most arrogant and confident people hold their hands at eye level, looking through the steeple at the other person.

If this steepling gesture is periodically alternated by a relaxed sitting posture, with both hands supporting the back of the head, the probability is increased that the seated person thinks of himself or herself as some kind of superior being. This gesture is recognized as an American gesture and is sometimes associated with relaxed aggression. When you discover relaxed aggression in conjunction with statements of superiority, you have made significant progress in deciphering an attitude.

Such gestures of superiority may be contrasted with ones reflecting uncertainty. Rather than steepling, people lacking confidence talk through their hands. They put their elbows on the table or desk and form a pyramid with their forearms. Alternatively, they hold both hands directly in front of the mouth.

This position is kept not only while talking but also while listening. It reflects shame or discomfort. As soon as people become more committed to what they are saying, they are likely to drop their hands from their mouths and place them firmly on the table. One may speculate that this gesture of uncertainty has grown from the habit of whispering with cupped hands.

On one occasion, while discussing an accounting procedure with a subordinate about which I was insecure, I recall using this hands-on-mouth gesture. I was embarrassed. My hands went up in front of my mouth, and I muttered feebly through them.

I remember being aware of my gesture, and I also remember making repeated efforts to move my hands away from my face. But each time, they would crawl back up to my face.

I realized then that to control this habit, I was going to require a good amount of practice. In my own mind, I questioned whether or not this effort was worthwhile. On one hand, I rationalized that the subordinate to whom I was talking probably was not even consciously aware of my insecurity. On the other hand, I was convinced that the sense of insecurity I projected through my gesture was apt to be registered at least subconsciously. If I was to command respect as a leader, I could not let myself behave in a way that reflected insecurity. Therefore, I decided that I had to gain some control over such involuntary gestures, even if it required significant work.

Some nonverbal signals, I should add here, seem to be beyond any conscious control. Among these are biological reactions and reflexes, which are purely subconscious. It is reported that some Yogis and people practicing with biofeedback machines have achieved control over some of these reflexes, but for our purposes, this possibility can be ignored.

The examples of such reflexes are numerous. When you are excited, your heartbeat accelerates. When you are nervous, you tend to perspire, and when you are frightened, your skin turns clammy. When you are angry, the blood pressure and body temperature rise, the face reddens, or brows become furrowed under tension. These are among the surest indicators of people's feelings.

Let us consider one of these strictly biological reflexes in more detail. As is well known, eye pupil dilation is beyond conscious control. You may force yourself to look at a person's face while talking, thereby pretending an interest that is not there, but you cannot consciously control the size of your eye pupils. The pupils change size automatically according to the amount of light to which they are exposed. If illumination is high, the pupils become small, and if illumination is low, they grow large.

However, it has been found by psychologists that the pupils

also change size with the *interest* that an individual feels. For example, if a woman is looking at a man and feels attracted to him, her pupils will dilate. Similarly, if a poker player has an exciting hand, his eye pupils will dilate.

Perhaps we could learn to control pupil dilation through biofeedback exercises, but the effect would probably be negligible. In any case, observation of this reflex can be a valuable tool for reading emotions.

Of course, we do not normally respond to variances in pupil size in any conscious way. For one thing, we rarely are familiar enough with an individual to know his or her normal pupil size. For another, we are often not close enough to others to be able to see the pupils.

However, we do respond to pupil dilation in an emotional way, even though we may not understand our reaction. In a famous experiment, people were asked to look at two nearly identical pictures of a person. The pictures differed in that in one of them, the size of the pupils was slightly enlarged. People regarded the picture with the more dilated pupil as more attractive.

In this experiment, the subjects were not aware how they arrived at their judgment, but one might speculate that the reason they found the more interested face more attractive was their natural vanity. Clearly, we all like to think of ourselves as deserving of interest, and it seems natural to expect that we are very sensitive to any sign of this emotion.

Experts who have studied subconscious eye gestures have noted other significant phenomena. For instance, they found that excessive eye blinking may be associated with a state of anxiety. It is as if people who are blinking their eyes at an abnormal rate were attempting to cut off reality. Psychiatrists have reported people blinking at rates of up to 100 times per minute, whereas normal blinking, needed to lubricate the eyeball, is measured at a rate of six to ten time per minute.

Although it is possible to force a blink, the consistent simulation of rapid blinking rates is as difficult as it is to force a shiver. Consequently, this behavioral response can be used as a valuable emotional indicator for anyone sensitive enough to such details.

An interesting problem concerning nonautomatic gestures—that is, ones that are not simple reflexes—is that although you are in principle able to control them, you are normally not aware of them. If that is the case, one is justified to ask why meaning should be inferred from them and where they come from.

Paul Ekman and Wallace Friesen speculate that there are three sources for our various nonverbal behaviors: (1) inherited neurologically-based expressions; (2) expressions common to all members of a particular species; and (3) expressions that vary with culture, class, family, or individuals.[3]

Many of these gestures may be rooted in early childhood, and some of them might even be associated with prenatal postures. Others may have been learned by copying the behavior of people who had some emotional influence on a particular individual, and this may occur at any stage of life. We are all prone to picking up various mannerisms from people whom we like or idolize. There are data, however, that indicate that at least some expressive facial patterns are not learned. This conclusion is supported, for instance, by the analysis of congenitally blind subjects, whose opportunities for learning facial expressions by imitation are clearly limited. Ekman and Friesen point out that if a congenitally blind man has never seen specific gesture patterns, he is likely to use them only if they are innate.

Finally, Ekman and Friesen suggest that some facial expressions may evolve in the same way for each individual not because of hereditary factors but as an extension of perfectly functional gestures. For instance, they suggest that the facial expression of disgust may have evolved from each person's movement of the mouth or nose in rejecting a bad taste or smell.

Gestures of space

The analysis of nonverbals would be incomplete without a consideration of the ways in which humans use space to express themselves.

The significance of space as an influential factor in nonverbal communication can be verified by simple observation of everyday life. Many people appreciate large houses, cars, property, shoulders, busts, and so on. There seems to be a majestic quality associated with largeness.

How powerful this factor can be is illustrated by an example from politics. It is reported that the tallest of two Presidential candidates seems to have been a consistent winner in American Presidential campaigns since 1900.[4] Another intriguing illustration of the principle is provided by a University of Pittsburgh study, which shows that graduates ranging in height from 6 feet 2 inches to 6 feet 4 inches received average starting salaries of 12.4 percent higher than those under 6 feet.[5]

Undoubtedly, our need for space is linked to a deep-seated subconscious mechanism. This can be verified by observing the behavior of groups in elevators or crowded buses and subway trains. Under these conditions of restricted space, even people who normally radiate a sense of authority often lose their personality and assume zombielike trances, totally ignoring the presence of other people.

The influence of space on our subconscious thinking is perhaps best explained as resulting from fear. For instance, the natural authority of tall people clearly seems to be linked to their physical power. After all, the "bully" or "king of the mountain" was usually the biggest of the group. Similarly, adults look large and threatening to children in their formative years, and therefore, it is not surprising that size is deeply associated in our subconscious with an authoritative position. Moreover, as children we feared being denied space; we tended to cry when put in the playpen or crib after an hour's adventure at breaking lamps.

On the other hand, we do not all react to space in the same way; rather, our relation to space is to some extent determined by our personalities. Some children can feel comfortable in a playpen, others can't. Introverts may require more space because they wish to be alone. People with inferiority complexes seem to feel that they are not worthy of occupying space. Extroverts, driven by their desire to be close to other people, will claim relatively little interpersonal space. Finally, individuals with a superiority complex will tend to use more space, regardless of their size.

It is interesting to observe how people will behave, whether or not they are aware of this, so as to create the interpersonal space they feel most comfortable with. The person with an inferiority complex will tend to keep his arms close to his body, thus occupying relatively little space, whereas the person who feels superior may keep his arms outstretched or locked behind the head, thereby keeping others at a distance.

We can generalize that the more important people feel, the more space they will occupy. In fact, the insistence on large cars and properties can be explained by noting that people use these props to increase the space they occupy and thereby artificially add to their demonstrable importance.

There are other, less obvious props that people use to increase the space they occupy. Examples include shoulder pads, Afro hairdos, high-rise shoes, but also strong colognes and even oil lotions that reflect light, thereby creating an illusion of extra space.

Similarly, someone who lets his coat fly open with total abandonment gives you a clear indication that he or she feels entitled to a maximum of space. And without props, somebody who drapes himself over a chair may be giving you the same signal.

In the office environment, charisma or importance is commonly associated with the use of space. Leaders often have bigger desks, offices, and even chairs.

I remember studying one individual in the Charleston, South Carolina, airport. He appeared to be particularly charismatic, but I could not link this quality to any of the conventional characteristics. His size, face, and dress were all quite normal.

After a while, I noted his shoes. They were big and shiny. For a long time my attention was fixed on them. Could they possibly generate a charismatic impression? Big shoes demand space, and shiny shoes reflect light, creating an added illusion of space. It was a possibility, yet I was not satisfied with it.

Then suddenly, I discovered how he really employed space to project leadership. He was using his associates to imply his importance. I am not sure that he was aware of what he was doing, but it was a magnificent psychological phenomenon.

He was the leader of a group of men—in a very simple, physical way. They followed him in his wanderings around the airport. He didn't always go first, but the group always maintained its physical relationship to him and among its members. There seemed to be a personal space around the charismatic individual that was much larger than the space between all the other members of the group. In fact, then, I was not looking at the charismatic individual alone but rather at the formation of the entire group.

We have seen, then, that the use of space can be a valuable clue to people's basic personalities. If they claim an unusual amount of interpersonal space, you may infer either that they are convinced of their own importance or else that they are of an introverted nature. Which of the two interpretations is the correct one must be determined by considering other aspects of their verbal and nonverbal behavior; in general, the distinction is obvious. Introverts will tend to be quiet and withdrawn, and their body gestures will be defensive rather than aggressive. To put it differently, you can create space between you and another person by jumping back like a frightened deer or by extending your arms to keep others at a distance.

But spacial gestures are indicators not only of people's basic personalities but also of their transitory feelings. For instance, a person who is normally self-confident may feel insecure in a particular situation, and this will be reflected in the way he or she occupies space. Therefore, reading spacial gestures is more than a tool for sizing up people's characters; it can be used to assess their changing attitudes toward you or a given situation.

Gestures of time

People's use of time is no less important than spatial gestures as an indicator of their feelings of confidence, aggression, inferiority, superiority, or anxiety. Examples of such gestures are numerous. For instance, whereas the subordinate will tend to be on time for a meeting, the superior may arrive late.

Similarly, if we were to measure the time that elapses between knocking and entering a room, we would probably find that the interval between the two events is determined by the hierarchical difference between the subordinate and the superior. If the superior comes to visit the subordinate, the delay will be minimal; in fact, the superior may enter the room without knocking at all. On the other hand, if the subordinate visits the superior, there may be a considerable interval between knocking and entering.

Another example is the time span that a person allows before answering a question. In general, subordinates tend to reply immediately, whereas superiors may take their time.

It is easy to see why such gestures of time are indicative of the subjective importance of people. Time is precious, and the more important we feel we are, the more jealous we are of our time. Hence, we feel that we cannot keep the superior waiting at our doorway or take his time as we deliberate over an intelligent answer. On the other hand, it seems perfectly all right for the superior to use the subordinate's time as he sucks on a pipe, thinking about the correct answer.

Such gestures of time are commonly used to reaffirm the superior-subordinate relationship, and as with space, their importance seems to be rooted in subconscious fears. Time is recognized as a valuable commodity, and we naturally strive for as much of it as possible. We want a long lifetime, and we want others to work or wait in line on our behalf. The more important you are, the more time you claim, and you obtain this extra time by taking it from others.

Of course, such gestures of time are open to misinterpretation. I may appear late for a meeting not because I want to assert my own importance but because I had trouble getting there on time. Similarly, I may pause before giving an answer simply because the question was complex and required a good deal of thought.

As with spacial gestures, however, the correct interpretation of gestures of time becomes obvious when they are considered in conjunction with other signals. For instance, a person who hesitates before venturing a reply will correctly be judged as an introvert if sitting with legs tightly crossed or nervously avoiding your eyes, but as arrogant if steepling or with a mocking smile on his or her face.

Using Nonverbals

Armed with a basic understanding of how to read nonverbals, you should not find it too difficult to learn how to use them effectively. In principle, they may be employed for two purposes: (1) to facilitate communication, and (2) to assert your leadership position.

Given the focus of this book, the second possibility is obviously of lesser importance to us. Synergistic management is most effective when it relies not on authority but on a team spirit that encourages trust and open communications. Nonetheless, to fulfill their control functions, managers, no matter what management style they adopt, must pay some attention to developing their leadership qualities, and we will therefore give some consideration to this aspect of nonverbal communication.

Gestures and postures

The first step in improving your body language is to analyze your own habits, in the same objective way in which you would interpret those of other people. Are your posture and gestures consistent with the image you want to project?

If you are shy, for instance, you may naturally stand straight with your arms folded across the chest, sit with your legs tightly crossed or on the edge of the chair, button your jacket, and talk through your hands. These are habits that are difficult to unlearn. You stand, sit, and gesture the way you do because you feel most comfortable with it.

In addition, it is not enough to control just one or two aspects of your bodily expressions. As will have become clear from the previous discussion, people judge you on the basis of whether or not your gestures and other nonverbal signals are consistent with each other and with what you say. Therefore, you must gain control over the totality of your verbal and nonverbal expressions, and this is obviously not easy to achieve.

Nonetheless, it can be done. Moreover, this is more than just an exercise in controlling superficial physical movements; it is an exercise of the mind as well. I believe that there is a close relationship between the ways you use your body, space, and time and the way you feel and think. Just as your nonverbal behavior is influenced by the state of your mind, so you can change your mental habits by altering your nonverbal behavior.

If you can force yourself to adopt a less guarded posture and more self-confident gestures, you can in fact change your personality style in a far-reaching way. The secret is to develop new *habits*, and this obviously requires some persistence. You must practice new postures and gestures until you feel comfortable with them; when this occurs, it will indicate that you have changed your frame of mind as well.

When the urge comes to button your jacket or hide your face behind your hands, resist it. When you catch yourself with your hands in your pockets, take them out. When you find that your eyes are straying away from people's faces, force yourself to look back at them. The more you practice this, the more natural it will become.

Once you gain control over a few basic postural and gestural habits, the rest will follow easily. As we discussed earlier, it is extremely difficult to exert conscious control over the totality of your body gestures. Picture yourself trying to start a sentence while telling yourself to hold your head upright, put your arms on your hips, spread your legs, smile, and relax your face.

If you are lucky enough to remember what you were about to say, chances are that you will overlook an important indicator that will give away your true feelings; you will be guilty of a postural or gestural Freudian slip.

The answer, as we said, is to develop a basic set of new habits that will make continuous conscious control unnecessary. If you have taught yourself to feel comfortable with a confident basic posture, secondary gestures that are consistent with this new habit will come automatically—they will simply become an integral part of your new personality.

The way I have practiced body language was by imagining myself in different personality profiles. Imagine yourself proud, successful, anxious, shy, aggressive, or pensive and note how certain muscles of the face and the body go along with these attitudes.

As you work at this while thinking about other things, you will notice that you begin to slip. Reposition yourself and try to keep up your posture. After some practice, you will find that less and less conscious effort is required to play this game. In this way, new postures and gestures may become a way of life for you in less than four weeks.

Using spatial gestures

People's use of space, as we have seen, is associated with their feelings of relative security and importance, as well as with their extroverted or introverted nature. The more superior you feel, the more space you will tend to occupy. Conversely, the more insecure or inferior you feel, the less space you will claim for yourself. Furthermore, if you are an extrovert, you are likely to put a minimum of distance between you and others, perhaps buttonholing them as you talk to them. If you are introverted, on the other hand, you will probably keep as far away from people as you can without having to shout.

Again, your first step must be self-analysis. Does your use of space indicate that you are excessively shy or unwilling to assert yourself? If you tend to nervously keep a distance from others, make it a habit to get closer to them. On the other hand, if you find that you are reluctant to create a reasonable amount of interpersonal space around yourself because of an irrational sense of inferiority, practice postures and gestures that are more open and self-confident. Don't sit on the edge of the chair and learn not to press your arms against the sides of your body as if you were stuck in an invisible sardine can.

To get there, all you have to do is to follow the advice given in the previous section. With enough practice, you will find that not just your spacial gestures change; your mental attitude changes as well.

Using gestures of time

This is by far the trickiest aspect of our subject. Although it is in principle possible to assert yourself and your position by claiming your share of time, it is easy to create ill feelings by overdoing this. People do not take lightly to your treating them as if their time were a cheap commodity, and intimidation techniques using gestures of time will usually be countered with hostility. Therefore, I would advise you to restrict your efforts essentially to interpreting other people's use of time.

With that warning in mind, however, it may well be worth your while to examine your habits in this area. Are you excessively timid in your use of time, to the point of choosing to give an answer without thinking? Clearly, this will do little for your cause, polite as it may be. Although it reflects a bad philosophy to show disrespect for other people's time, there is no reason why you should not insist on your fair share too.

There is another aspect to this problem of defending your share of time. We have probably all experienced the situation where people visit our office, talk business, and then light up a cigarette or sit back and relax and start a personal conversation. This is their way of indicating that they are going to take a break, regardless of your own situation.

Frequently, this poses a real dilemma. Clearly, it would be bad form to say, "Please leave my office." On the other hand, we may simply not have the time for a friendly chat, and therefore, we must take steps to induce the other person to leave.

Some managers deal with such situations in a wholesale way, namely by using props to discourage people from lingering on.

They often brag about purposefully having no comfortable chair or no ashtray in their office.

Although this may work, it is a lazy, undifferentiated approach that does not allow you to adjust to specific needs. Clearly, there will be times when you want people to stay in your office, and furthermore, they should be comfortable while being with you, or they will be ineffective listeners.

It is preferable, therefore, to resort to more flexible postural or gestural signals in cases where you wish to be left alone. You may push your chair back to indicate that you are about to leave your office, pick up some work and casually glance at it, or simply stand up and extend your hand. The key is to spot the *early* signs of relaxation in your visitor and take action before the situation becomes too obvious.

Conclusion

Nonverbals, as we have seen, are more than an insignificant background to speech. They can be powerful indicators of unexpressed feelings and of people's characters. Knowing how to read them gives you a valuable tool for sizing up people's personalities and reactions, and that knowledge can be put to use to make the goal of synergy a reality.

It isn't easy. But if you persist in your efforts, you can increase your sensitivity to these signals, and you can unlearn old habits and acquire a more assertive and open personality. In the end, you may know more about your people, see their strengths and weaknesses in a clearer light, and learn to influence their behavior in ways that would have seemed impossible to you before.

The secrets are a healthy degree of self-analysis, perseverance, and an open mind. But aren't those just the qualities we can expect of a good manager anyhow?

You may well decide—be it for personal reasons or because you feel that your business environment is not ripe for it—that synergistic management is not a realistic goal for you. As I said, there *are* risks, and they must be weighed carefully against the benefits that you hope to gain from synergy. Still, even if you cannot commit yourself to the total concept, I hope that some of the ideas in this book will prove useful to you.

NOTES

1. Mehrabian, Albert, and Susan R. Ferris, "Inference of Attitudes from Nonverbal Communication in Two Channels," *Journal of Consulting Psychology* 31, (1967), pp. 248–252.
2. Birdwhistell, Ray L., *Kinesics and Context*, Philadelphia: University of Pennsylvania Press, 1970.
3. Ekman, Paul, and Wallace V. Friesen, "The Repertoire of Nonverbal Behavior: Categories, Origins, and Coding," *Semiotica* 1 (1969), pp. 49–98.
4. Knapp, Mark L., *Nonverbal Communications in Human Interaction*, New York: Holt, Rinehart and Winston, 1972.
5. Ibid.

Index